Spatial Neglect

A clinical handbook for diagnosis and treatment

Ian H. Robertson
Trinity College Dublin, Ireland

Peter W. Halligan
University of Oxford
Rivermead Rehabilitation Centre, Oxford

Psychology Press
a member of the Taylor & Francis group

Psychology Press Ltd, Publishers
27 Church Road
Hove
East Sussex, BN3 2FA,
UK

British Library Cataloguing-in-Publication Data

A catalogue record for this book is available from the British Library

    ISBN 0-86377-809-7 (hbk)
    ISBN 0-86377-810-0 (pbk)
    ISSN 0967-9944

Typeset by Quorum Technical Services Ltd, Cheltenham, Glos.
Printed and bound in the UK by Biddles Ltd, Guildford and King's Lynn

The two pictures on the front cover are pre- and post-stroke drawings of a cat.

Contents

Acknowledgements

We would like to gratefully acknowledge the considerable help given generously by the following colleagues in preparing this book: Professor J.C. Marshall, Dr D.T. Wade, Dr Jennie Ponsford, Dr Nadina Lincoln, Mrs Julia Darling, Mrs V. Berry, and C.M. Keane, o.p.

Brain Damage, Behaviour and Cognition:
Developments in Clinical Neuropsychology
Titles in Series

Series Preface

From being an area primarily on the periphery of mainstream behavioural and cognitive science, neuropsychology has developed in recent years into an area of central concern for a range of disciplines. We are witnessing not only a revolution in the way in which brain–behaviour–cognition relationships are viewed, but a widening of interest concerning developments in neuropsychology on the part of a range of workers in a variety of fields. Major advances in brain-imaging techniques and the cognitive modelling of the impairments following brain damage promise a wider understanding of the nature of the representation of cognition and behaviour in the damaged and undamaged brain.

Neuropsychology is now centrally important for those working with brain-damaged people, but the very rate of expansion in the area makes it difficult to keep up with findings from current research. The aim of the *Brain Damage, Behaviour and Cognition* series is to publish a wide range of books that present comprehensive and up-to-date overviews of current developments in specific areas of interest.

These books will be of particular interest to those working with the brain-damaged. It is the editors' intention that undergraduates, postgraduates, clinicians and researchers in psychology, speech pathology and medicine will find this series a useful source of information on important current developments. The authors and editors of the books in this series are experts in their respective fields, working at the forefront of contemporary research. They have produced texts that are accessible and scholarly. We thank them for their contribution and their hard work in fulfilling the aims of the series.

CC and GH
Sydney, Australia and Birmingham, UK
Series Editors

CHAPTER ONE

Clinical presentation of spatial neglect

INTRODUCTION

Many patients who survive brain damage are left with a variety of cognitive difficulties which can adversely affect their recovery and treatment. The term "cognitive" is used here to describe a wide range of mental abilities including perception, reasoning, memory, and language. Cognitive impairments are often missed or poorly described in clinical practice, yet they often influence the patient's recovery and may explain the patient's failure to respond adequately to rehabilitation. As many types of everyday cognitive activities involve directing attention to selective spatial features of our environment, it is not surprising that visuospatial disorders after brain damage are sometimes difficult to identify or characterise.

Adequate visual perception and spatial perception is necessary, however, for most daily activities, e.g. dressing, object manipulation, drawing, finding one's way about, reading, walking and acquiring new motor skills. The importance of visuospatial disturbances has tended to be underestimated, involving as they do the location of the person with respect to the world and its objects, and the relation of these objects to each other. These disorders, which are commonly encountered after right hemisphere stroke, have been shown to constitute a substantial impairment for functional recovery. Furthermore, they can limit the effectiveness of rehabilitation, often to a greater extent than more obvious motor, sensory, and speech deficits (Halligan & Cockburn, 1993). Evidence from several stroke studies indicates that the most disruptive and common visuospatial symptom after right-sided stroke remains unilateral (visual) neglect—the focus of this book.

Although unilateral visual neglect, or hemi-inattention, represents one of the most common visuospatial disorders, it still remains poorly understood. In this book, we focus on the clinical assessment and rehabilitation of visual neglect. Although the book will provide a general overview of current research findings, the intention is not to replicate recent specialised texts concerned with the theoretical mechanisms thought to explain the condition. For a comprehensive review of the neuropsychology of neglect, the interested reader is directed to Bradshaw and Mattingley (1996); Halligan and Marshall (1994d); Heilman, Watson, and Valenstein (1993); McCarthy and Warrington (1990); Robertson and Marshall (1993); Jeannerod (1987); and Weinstein and Friedland (1977b).

WHAT IS NEGLECT?

Unilateral neglect or hemi-inattention are clinical terms used by neurologists, neuropsychologists, and therapists to describe a family of often different behavioural symptoms characterised by the patient's failure to attend or respond to objects or people in selective parts of space. The term "neglect" has often been used imprecisely to cover a host of sensory, perceptual, and attentional deficits. When used to describe the clinical condition that typically follows right brain damage, the term describes the failure to report, respond, or orient to novel or meaningful stimuli—usually, but not always, on the side of space or objects opposite the side of the lesion. The term "neglect" cannot be meaningfully used if the target behaviours can be explained by either primary sensory or motor deficits (Heilman et al., 1993). Within clinical practice, unilateral neglect was initially considered to be a single syndrome (Heilman et al., 1993). However, the set of behaviours attributed to this syndrome suggests that it is unlikely to be a unitary disorder and many different types of neglect have now been described (Halligan & Marshall, 1994d).

Neglect failed to receive serious theoretical and clinical interest until the late 1970s, due in part to the implicit assumption that it could somehow be explained by the patient's failure to compensate for more obvious sensory and motor problems. Neglect, however, is more than a visual field cut, hearing loss, or motor weakness. Many "neglect behaviours" cannot be adequately explained in terms of sensory or motor loss. Although many patients do indeed have visual field deficits and hemiplegia, severe neglect can be seen in patients without such deficits. Furthermore, the lesions that produce visual neglect are not necessarily limited to the primary sensory or motor areas of the brain.

As many patients with neglect believe that they have an adequate perception of the world, the necessity to make adjustments such as turning their heads to look and search for missing objects on the affected side is not obvious. Consequently such patients often present with additional problems of minimisation, rationalisation, denial, and/or confusion.

In the absence of adequate primary sensory or motor explanations, a variety of neuropsychological accounts have been put forward to explain the condition; most of these characterise the condition as a set of *attentional disorders*, although other explanations emphasise perceptual, representational, intentional, and pre-motor factors. These accounts no longer consider explanations in terms of a disorder of seeing, hearing, feeling or moving but rather one that involves a disturbance of looking, listening, touching, and exploring space (Mesulam, 1981).

CLINICAL DESCRIPTIONS

Throughout the book, the typical illustrations of left neglect after right brain damage (RBD) are adopted. Patients with neglect often collide with objects on their left side, fail to eat from the left side of the plate, and dress only one side of the body. Illustrations of this striking behaviour in the case of drawing are shown in this chapter. Clinically, visual neglect is often associated in the acute phase with a marked deviation of the head, eyes, and trunk towards the side of lesion. In more serious cases, patients fail to recognise their contralateral extremities as their own, and only attend to those events and people situated on the ipsilesional side. Neglect may encompass several sensory modalities and involve aspects of personal, extrapersonal, and representational space. Many patients, not surprisingly, show difficulties in reading, written arithmetic, writing, and drawing as a result.

For many patients, visual neglect is not a transitory problem. A study by Kinsella and Ford (1985) showed that the effects of visual neglect can persist up to 18 months post stroke. Features of neglect can continue to be insidiously disruptive in many areas of the patient's daily life long after the resolution of florid symptoms. Zarit and Kahn (1974) reported features of neglect up to 12 years post stroke. The persistence of visual neglect has significant ramifications, as stroke patients comprise a large proportion of those treated in hospital and rehabilitation centres. Many of these patients require close supervision in daily activities, as they are particularly prone to accidents. Visual neglect limits, therefore, the degree of active participation in retraining programs and is commonly associated with poor functional recovery.

To provide the reader with a clinical picture of the complex presentation of neglect, we present four cases that help illustrate the range of neglect phenomena commonly seen after right brain damage.

Case 1: John

Clinical presentation.   John is a right-handed businessman who suffered a stroke that affected movement on the left side of his body. Before his stroke, John suffered from angina and had been treated for hypertension. John's stroke paralysed his left leg and arm and cut off vision on the left side. John now complains that he cannot see the nurses or doctors when they talk to him on his left side. A CT scan (Fig. 1.1) showed a large area of damage located on the right side of his brain. Over the next four weeks, John's arm and leg began to improve slowly; however, nursing staff at the hospital noticed that John's most disabling problem was his apparent unawareness of people and objects located on his left side.

Behavioural observations.   On the ward, John could be seen searching for his spectacles which were in fact located on the left side of the table in front of him. His hand feels along the surface of the tabletop but never quite makes the last 6 inches (on his left) which separates him from his glasses. Despite several head turns to the left, his eyes appear to scan only those objects located on the right side of the table. When the nurse approaches from his left and asks John if he has filled out his menu card for the week's meals, he initially fails to respond to her, even though his hearing is otherwise normal. When the nurse calls his name loudly several times, he does eventually, but slowly, move his eyes and head round in small jerky movements and replies to her. When

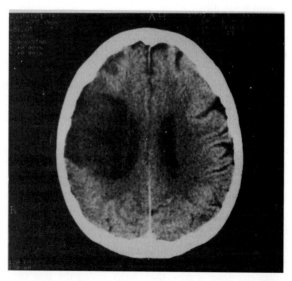

FIG. 1.1   CT scan (right on left) of John's brain after his stroke (Case 1).

requested to look further to his left, John eventually finds his glasses; while picking them up, he notices the menu card which had been lying immediately to the left of them. He reads from the menu card but as the days' choices are lined up from the left side of the card, John checks only those items from Friday through Sunday, leaving Monday to Thursday blank. Finally, when his food does arrive he also misses the potato on the left side of his plate (see Fig. 1.2 for a typical illustration).

When he writes letters to friends, John often squeezes the text over to the right side of the page. An example of his writing performance is shown in Fig. 1.3. When dialling a telephone number that had been written down by a friend, John is surprised and frustrated by the frequency of the wrong numbers he gets. Although John can be made aware of his neglect in this and other situations, he nevertheless continues to make similar errors and often attempts to explain his problems in terms of others forgetting or equipment that does not work. Recently, he was particularly upset to find out that on several occasions over the previous week, he had totally ignored his two favourite grandchildren; they had been playing on the floor 6–8 feet away from him—on his left side!

John announces he is going to the toilet, but as he tries to back his wheelchair out from the table there is a loud metallic noise. He looks down to his right while repeatedly pushing the chair out with his leg. The obstruction is on the left side of his wheelchair. When this is pointed out to him by a nurse, he slowly looks over to his left and discovers the problem for the first time. Only then does he manage to extract himself and proceed through the ward towards the toilet. A few minutes later, there is a series of minor accidents as John collides his wheelchair into a door-post, a cabinet, and a fellow patient's wheelchair, all located on his left side. Furthermore, having taken only right turns on the way to the toilet, John now finds himself totally lost. With some difficulty, he is directed to the toilet.

FIG. 1.2   Food neglected on the left side of plate.

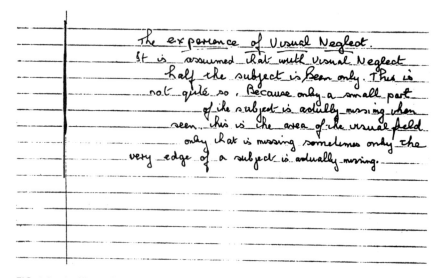

FIG. 1.3   An illustration of neglect dysgraphia: Writing is squeezed over to the right side of the page. Reproduced with permission from Halligan, P.W., and Robertson, I. (1992). The assessment of unilateral neglect. In J.R. Crawford, D.M. Parker & W.W. McKinlay (Eds.), *A handbook of neuropsychological assessment* (p. 159). Hove, UK: Lawrence Erlbaum Associates Ltd.

Another noticeable aspect of John's behaviour is that he is prone to lapses of attention; his concentration appears to "drift off" during a task. This happens particularly in therapy sessions, where he has to be constantly reminded to attend to the exercises or tasks he is doing. His relatives also notice that he has difficulty following conversations when they are talking to him or when he is watching television.

Case 2: Rachel

Clinical presentation.   Rachel is a 59-year-old school teacher who suffered a stroke three weeks previously. She suffered a large middle cerebral artery stroke, resulting in a mild left paralysis affecting her leg more than her arm. She has some sensation in her left arm, but shows marked sensory extinction (i.e. poor detection of left stimuli in the presence of right stimuli) when tested on double simultaneous stimulation. Her visual fields were full to confrontation testing. However, she also shows visual extinction when bilateral objects are presented simultaneously in her visual fields.

Behavioural observations.   Most of the time, Rachel's eyes and head are turned to her right-hand side; she appears unable to relax her neck muscles to allow her head to flex towards the hemiplegic side. Seated in her wheelchair,

Rachel adopts a posture where her trunk is flexed; her head is turned to the right and most of the activities she engages in are located on her right side. When she copies (Fig. 1.4) she misses out many of the relevant features on the left side.

On one occasion, Rachel wheels herself into the day room when she suddenly comes to a stop. Her left foot has become twisted under the foot plate and has started rubbing against the floor. Rachel can only extricate her leg with help. In addition, the nurse has to remind Rachel to lift up her paralysed left arm which is hanging limply down her side with her fingers dangling dangerously close to the spinning spokes of the wheel.

Once in the day room, Rachel fumbles in her handbag for her spectacles and, when she finally puts them on, the left spectacle-arm is caught in her hair and never positioned correctly behind her left ear. After several minutes, the skewed spectacles are straightened by a member of staff. Rachel's husband and the nursing staff notice that she only puts on lipstick and make-up on the right side of her face, that her hair is often tangled and unkempt on the left side, and that she complains regularly that personal toiletries of hers have gone missing—all of which were on her left!

Case 3: Victor

Clinical presentation.   Victor is a 65-year-old retired mechanic who suffered a large fronto-parietal stroke, complete left-sided hemiplegia, and loss of vision on the left side (left homonymous hemianopia) 1 month previously.

FIG. 1.4   Rachel's copy of a figure, showing neglect of the left side (see Case 2).

Figure 1.5 shows a chart of Victor's visual field; the blind areas of his visual fields are located on the left side.

Behavioural observations. The most striking aspect of Victor's behaviour remains the apparent lack of awareness that there is anything wrong with him. Victor is forever asking staff why he can't go home, insisting that he is perfectly capable of looking after himself. When reminded that his left side is paralysed, he replies that it is just a little weak and that this has resulted from lack of use and from being confined to his bed and wheelchair. When asked to lift his left arm, he replies that he can do this but that he can't be bothered to do it now—as he is too tired. When asked to reach over and touch his left arm with his right, he begins but stops short around the middle of his body.

Victor can't find his hand towel which is lying on the left side of his bed. He looks round to his right and back again, this time noticing the towel. He grumbles to a passing therapist about people playing tricks on him by continually taking his things and then putting them back in different places when he is not looking. When Victor tries to read, he is forever changing his spectacles, on and off in a repetitive cycle. He continually blames his spectacles for not being able to read the newspaper and watch TV anymore.

Case 4: Veronica

Clinical presentation. Veronica is a 55-year-old part-time senior NHS administrator who suffered a mild stroke which primarily affected her walking and balance. She has full movement on her left side, and her visual fields are normal. Sensation on the left side has been mildly affected by the stroke. Furthermore, although she shows visual and tactile extinction when stimuli are presented simultaneously, sometimes when her left arm is touched out of sight, she reports a feeling of being touched on a similar location on the right-hand side.

Behavioural observations. Veronica shows some of the symptoms of the first two cases described earlier. Although she has full use of her limbs, she nevertheless often fails to notice things on her left side. On some occasions, Veronica attributes sensory stimulation on her left side to stimulation on her opposite side. However, her main concern relates to reading and writing difficulties, which she complains to the clinical psychologist and occupational therapist about. She claims that she has difficulty concentrating on text; she gives up reading after just a couple of lines because the text does not appear to make sense. When asked to read aloud from a favourite book, she regularly omits to read the full width of the lines of text. On some occasions it is apparent that she is "filling in" the omitted words in order to make sense of what she is reading. She frequently misreads single words; e.g. reading *ball* as "hall", *match* as

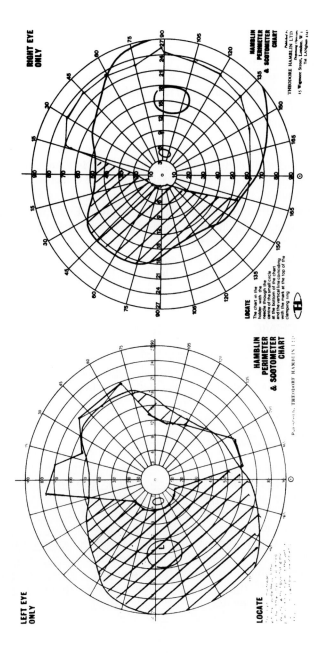

FIG 1.5   Victor's visual field chart for left and right eyes (see Case 3). The shaded areas represent the areas of visual loss.

"hatch", and *heel* as "eel". Figure 1.6 shows an example of her reading performance. In addition, when asked to spell from memory words that are clearly familiar to her, she again tends to omit the left side of the word. When writing to dictation she crams all the text to one side, omits words, and shows a tendency to repeat letters within words.

All these problems have severely reduced her ability to read and continue her duties as a senior administrative officer. Similar problems occur in writing.

Summary and further information

It is hoped that the clinical details of these four cases will help clinicians unfamiliar with neglect to gain some insight into the presentation of the condition. Helping such patients to cope successfully with the effects of their stroke requires the recognition, not only of their physical problems, but also of the less obvious and just as disabling effects of their neglect. Examples of neglect behaviour in drawing tasks and the experience of what it feels like to have neglect from a patient's perspective can be found in two teaching videos entitled "Illustrations of Visual Neglect" and "The Experience of Visual Neglect", both of which are available from Psychology Press (ISBN: 086377-3230).

CLINICAL RELEVANCE OF NEGLECT

As we can see from the four cases described earlier, patients with unilateral left-sided neglect following right brain damage can experience severe problems, many of which can disrupt basic daily activities. The significance of

---

Perceptual Aspects of Unilateral Neglect

In patients with unilateral neglect, sensory events within the left extrapersonal hemispace appear to lose their impact on awareness, especially when competing events are taking place in the other half of the extrapersonal world. The most obvious demonstration of this occurs when patients who respond perfectly well to unilateral stimulation from either the left or the right side consistently ignore the stimulation on the left under conditions of bilateral simultaneous stimulation. Especially when it occurs in more than one modality, the phenomenon of sensory extinction suggests that the left hemispace is neglected, even though the brain receives the relevant elementary sensory information.

FIG. 1.6   Veronica's neglect in text reading (see Case 4): The underlined text is the text she read. Text reproduced with permission from Mesulam, M.M. (1985) *Principles of behavioral neurology* (p. 142). Philadelphia, PA: F.A. Davis Company.

spatial disturbances such as neglect lies in their functional and behavioural consequences. Studies have shown that neglect contributes to the poor recovery by limiting the effectiveness of rehabilitation. Neglect is associated with poor functional recovery in reading, writing, and basic self-care skills (Denes, Semenza, Stoppa, & Lis, 1982; Halligan & Cockburn, 1993). Some areas affected by neglect are shown in Table 1.1.

A follow-up study by Kinsella and Ford (1980, 1985) using the Northwick Park Activities of Daily Living (NPADL) index, showed how the presence of neglect significantly influenced the progress of patients with right hemisphere stroke. Figure 1.7 shows the mean scores for individual test items on the NPADL index at 4, 8, and 12 weeks post stroke, while Fig. 1.8 shows the same means scores at 15/18 months post stroke.

Reports of the incidence of neglect vary considerably, depending on number and type of the tests used, the type of pathology, the impairment criteria employed, and the length of time post stroke onset. A selection of studies and their respective incidence figures are shown in Fig. 1.9.

Each of the four patients described earlier illustrate some of the characteristic features and clinical types of neglect commonly encountered after stroke and in some cases of head injury. Box 1.1 describes the long-term clinical significance of unilateral neglect.

Visual neglect is qualitatively distinct from other visual neuropsychological phenomena such as visual agnosia or disorientation, which take for granted the spatial medium in which to manifest. Patients with florid neglect are distinctive in that their problem is not simply one of an inability to see objects on one half of space, but in many cases an inability to conceive of space on that side and therefore be aware of the errors involved. This aspect of neglect behaviour in an

TABLE 1.1

Examples of everyday neglect behaviours shown by neglect patients

Increase in the number of accidents while walking/negotiating wheelchair
Difficulties crossing the road, transferring from a wheelchair, handling money, phoning, watching TV, and eating food
Difficulty reading the time from a clock face
Failing to shave or dress the left side of the body; applying make-up to one side
Missing food on the left side of the plate
Failing to read the left side of words or sentences when reading the newspaper
Omitting the left parts of words or sentences when copying or writing text
Confining written text or drawings to the right side of the page
Bumping into doorways and staff while walking or using wheelchair
Failing to take relevant right-sided turns and often getting lost while travelling between hospital departments
Failing to notice family or friends located on the affected side
Complaints of having lost personal items located on the left

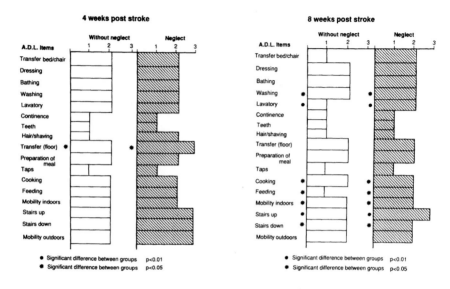

FIG. 1.7   Recovery of everyday functions on a standard ADL index for neglect and non-neglect stroke patients at 4 and 8 weeks post stroke. (Adapted from Kinsella & Ford, 1980).

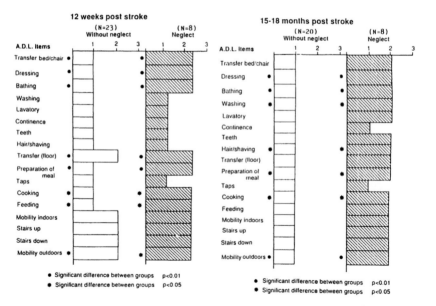

FIG. 1.8   Recovery of everyday functions on a standard ADL index for neglect and non-neglect stroke patients at 12 weeks and 15–18 months post stroke. (Adapted from Kinsella & Ford, 1980, 1985).

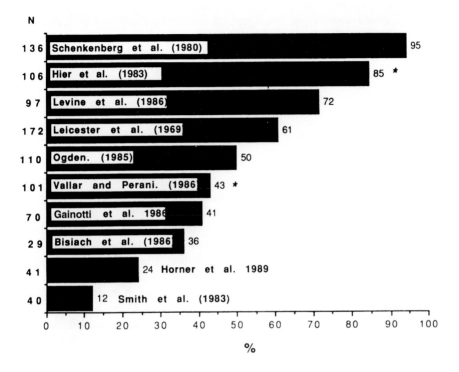

FIG. 1.9   A graphic illustration of the variable incidence of visual neglect.

BOX 1.1   Prognosis for neglect patients

How can we predict who recovers well from a stroke and who will not? Several studies have attempted to address this question using neuropsychological measures to predict the ability to relearn walking, self-care and other important everyday living (ADL) skills. Studies by Denes et al. (1982) and Gialanella and Mattioli (1992) found that the presence of unilateral neglect was the single strongest predictor of motor recovery. Other studies by Fullerton, Mackenzie, and Stout (1988) and Stone, Patel, Greenwood, & Halligan (1992) have shown similar results. In the latter case, Stone et al. (1992) devised a "visual neglect recovery index" (VNRI) capable of expressing the amount of neglect on a battery of tests as a percentage of complete recovery from maximal neglect measurable. Severity of neglect at 3 months and at 6 months could be predicted by the severity of visual neglect and the presence of anosognosia at 2/3 days. These authors supply a predictive equation for use by clinicians interested in randomising patients for intensive treatment.

otherwise well oriented and intelligent patient creates additional difficulties for recovery and militates against involvement and success in many therapy programmes. In most cases these difficulties are caused by several different types of neglect. In this section we outline the main clinically recognised types of neglect behaviour.

"NEGLECT SYNDROME"

It is already clear from the large amount of recent research that unilateral neglect is not a single deficit but constitutes several related deficits, all of which demonstrate a predominantly lateralised disorder of attention when using and working in space. Although different neglect symptoms may occur on their own and may recover at different rates, there is a general consensus among clinicians that the various conditions constitute a "clinical syndrome" that reflects a disruption of different brain areas responsible for deploying attention in contralesional space (Stone, Halligan, Marshall, & Greenwood, 1998). One of the most striking features of neglect is that it is much more common and severe following right brain damage than left brain damage. Indeed, it is the most common neuropsychological deficit to follow right hemisphere brain damage (Stone, Halligan, & Greenwood, 1993). Box 1.2 outlines some possible reasons for this asymmetry.

The "neglect syndrome" has been used to describe a family of clinically related symptoms all of which share the patient's failure to respond to sounds, objects, or touch on the side opposite their lesion. Since the severity and extent of strokes vary, it is not the case that all patients show all the disorders listed here. The neglect syndrome first described by Heilman et al. (1993) is divided into several components: hemi-inattention, hemispatial neglect, extinction, allesthesia, anosognosia, and hemiakinesia. The latter will be discussed under motor neglect.

Hemi-inattention and hemispatial neglect

Lacking a clear definition, these two terms are often used interchangeably in practice. Hemi-inattention refers to a general lack of awareness for one side of space and can often be seen by simply observing the patient's general sponta-neous behaviour during most everyday activities. It has been used to describe the general condition whereby the patient fails to direct their attention sponta-neously or respond to objects on one side (i.e. hemi) when listening, feeling, or seeing unless attention is explicitly drawn to that space or to the objects concerned. Typical examples of hemi-inattention include failing to notice people approaching from one side and consistently bumping into obstacles or

BOX 1.2 Why is left neglect more common than right?

Neglect and its related problems are more common after right than left brain damage. This asymmetry has led to several hypotheses concerning hemispheric specialisation for perceptuo-attentional processes. Central to Kinsbourne's (1987) influential account of neglect is the assumption of two mutually antagonistic vectors which direct attention to opposite sides of space. Although each is capable of producing enhanced attention to contralateral space, the left hemisphere is relatively stronger. Kinsbourne argues that activational imbalance is produced by hemispheric brain damage and it is this that determines the directional vector that controls attentional orienting bias. In other words, the failure of the right hemisphere to inhibit the left hemisphere leaves the strong rightward orienting tendency of the intact hemisphere unopposed and so produces left-sided neglect. Left-sided orientational bias after lesions of the left hemisphere are inherently weaker due to the strong bilateral coverage of the intact right hemisphere. Consequently, directional right-sided neglect is both rare and less severe. A related hypothesis, by Mesulam (1981), proposes that the right hemisphere is dominant for the deployment of attention to all spatial locales. Attentional neurons in the right cerebral hemisphere have bilateral receptive fields while those in the left are exclusively concerned with contralesional space. Consequently, damage to the right hemisphere should result not only in contralesional neglect but also some degree of neglect for ipsilateral space. The left hemisphere requires assistance from the right hemisphere in order to attend fully to right-sided space. By contrast, damage to the left hemisphere should result in relatively mild contralesional neglect. The right hemisphere therefore, is regarded as dominant for spatial attention in that it makes a larger overall contribution to the neural representation of space; it is capable of directing attention to any part of space, and has a slight bias towards contralateral space. The left hemisphere makes a smaller overall contribution, but is strongly biased towards contralateral space.

doorways on one side. Sometimes Victor (Case 3, pp. 7–8), ignores the doctor when she speaks to him on his impaired side. When, however, she walks around to his non-affected side he would often respond to her as if she had just arrived.

Hemispatial neglect, on the other hand, tends to be elicited on formal tests or in the course of careful observation of the patient in certain everyday activities. In practice, however, we acknowledge the imprecision of both terms and simply use the term "neglect" to describe the first two components of the neglect syndrome outlined above.

Neglect can be easily seen on a variety of simple bedside tasks. These include drawing and copying, reading, dividing a line in half (line bisection), and crossing out specific targets on a page (cancellation). Figure 1.10 shows examples of some of these problems. On drawing a flower the patient with neglect typically fails to draw the left side; on a cancellation task, the patient

(a)

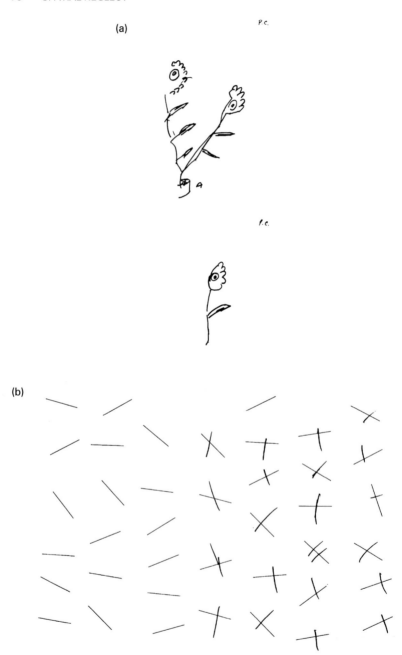

FIG 1.10   Left-sided neglect on tests of copying (a) and cancellation (b).

misses out letters on the left side; when asked to divide a line length in half, the patient puts a mark that is considerably skewed to the right of the actual centre.

Most patients when requested to draw or copy, commonly complain that their drawing/copying skills were never very good to start with. Consequently, when artists present with neglect after right brain damage, there are premorbid drawings or artwork with which it is possible to compare their neglect work. Box 1.3 describes and illustrates some established artists who were affected by neglect as a result of their stroke.

Extinction and allesthesia

Extinction describes a condition whereby a patient who can reliably see or feel an object on the side opposite their brain damage when one stimulus is used, fails to see or feel the *same* stimulus when a similar stimulus is simultaneously presented on the non-affected side. For instance, Veronica (Case 4, pp. 8–10) reported that she could see single objects moving on her left side when she was looking straight ahead and with no other movement to distract her. However, when her attention was directed to an object positioned on the right-hand side at

---

BOX 1.3   Art and neglect

The drawings of several graphic artists have been affected by neglect after stroke. One of the best illustrations of neglect recovery is the four self-portraits made by the German artist Anton Raderscheidt, at 2, 4, 6 and 9 months after his stroke (Wertz, Goldberg, & Robinson, 1982). Howard Gardner in his book "Art, Mind and Brain: A Cognitive Approach to Creativity" (1982) illustrates how the work of Lovis Corinth, another famous German painter, was influenced by neglect after his stroke in 1911.

In 1990, one of the authors (PWH), together with John C. Marshall, had the opportunity to see at first hand some of the effects of neglect on the work of the distinguished artist Tom Greenshields, after his stroke in 1989. Tom, who was born in 1915, was the grandson of the Victorian painter Edouard van Goethem and had trained at the Slade School of Art, in London. Despite losing the use of his right arm in a farming accident in 1981, Tom successfully transferred his artistic skills to his left hand and continued to exhibit his paintings, and in particular his sculptures, in many galleries in the UK. After his stroke, in addition to other visuo-constructive problems, Tom was initially unable to attend to the left part of his drawings and sculptures (Halligan & Marshall, 1997). An example (Fig. 1.11) illustrates this effect.

A teaching video that illustrates some of Tom's artistic work before and after his stroke, entitled "Art and visuospatial perception: The effect of stroke on a graphic artist", is available from Psychology Press (ISBN: 086377-3230). Using examples from his pre-stroke drawings and sculpture, this video traces Tom's recovery whilst demonstrating the effects of visual neglect on his artistic productions after the stroke. Tom died in August 1994.

(a)

(b)

FIG. 1.11   Pre- and post-stroke drawings by the artist Tom Greenshields.

the same time, she only reported the right-sided object. Rachel (Case 2, pp. 6–7) showed tactile extinction: i.e. she could feel a single touch on her left arm but not when there was a similar touch on her right arm at the same time. Only patients who are able to reliably report unilateral left-sided stimulation and who do not suffer contralesional sensory loss can be validly tested. Extinction has been regarded as a mild form of neglect which becomes evident with recovery. Extinction can be found in hearing, seeing, and feeling. Frequently extinction only becomes obvious after recovery from hemi-inattention because it remains untestable while the latter is present. Unlike neglect, it has to be tested for using double simultaneous stimulation.

Allesthesia refers to the tendency to mislocate stimuli presented on the affected side to various different positions on the non-affected side. Veronica (Case 4), for instance, demonstrated allesthesia on several occasions, e.g. when she was touched by the doctor on her left shoulder, she often maintained that she felt the sensation on her right arm. Allesthesia is the term used to describe this false mislocalisation of stimuli to the non-affected side of the body. Allesthesia can also include instances where the patient responds to something seen on the left as if it is on the right. Alternatively, some patients when requested to mark in the main cities or towns located on the left (west) side of a map may transpose these towns/cities to a more eastern coastline. An illustration of John's attempts to mark cities on a map of the British Isles is shown in Fig. 1.12 (see Case 1, pp. 4–6).

When Veronica (Case 4) was asked to write her name with a pen lying on her left side, she was seen to reach out with her right hand to a space on the right of her body. Allocusis is the term used to describe the same phenomena when it occurs in hearing. In the early stages after his stroke, John (Case 1) was reported by care staff to be responding to relatives' questions which had come from his left as if they had come from his right side.

Anosognosia

Victor (Case 3), appears unaware of the effects of his stroke and consequently attempts to explain his situation by minimising or denying his problems. He does not realise that he does not see things located on the left and also appears unaware of the fact that he has suffered a severe paralysis on his left side. This apparent lack of awareness for the effects of the stroke is called anosognosia. There is no generally accepted explanation or test for anosognosia, but the condition is regarded as a disorder of conscious awareness secondary to brain damage (Prigatano & Schacter, 1991). Anosognosia is commonly associated with visual neglect in the early stages of the condition, although the two conditions are not the same. Patients may demonstrate neglect but not anosognosia and vice versa. In severe cases, anosognosia can manifest itself in the patients' failure to recognise their affected limbs as their own. Anosodiaphoria is

FIG. 1.12   Mislocation of Irish cities and towns eastwards (allesthesia) onto the UK mainland by a patient with neglect.

considered to be a milder condition of impaired awareness, often seen in previ-ously anosognosic patients who now recognise with recovery some of their impairments and disabilities. The term, however, describes the patients' apparent indifference and lack of appropriate affect when confronted with the striking effects of their stroke. We know that anosognosia is a key reason why neglect is so strongly predictive of poor outcome following right hemisphere stroke (Gialanella & Mattioli, 1992; Stone, Patel, Greenwood, & Halligan, 1992). Yet there is relatively little research on anosognosia, and different accounts have been put forward to explain it (Prigatano & Schacter, 1991).

MOTOR FEATURES OF NEGLECT

Although most neglect phenomena have been explained in terms of a failure to attend or perceive objects located on one side of space, recent research has indicated that pre-motor movement processes may also play a significant role. There is now growing evidence that neglect can be subdivided in terms of two broad categories: (1) disorders of inattention (perceptual neglect) and (2) disorders of action (motor) and/or inattention (pre-motor neglect). Inattentional neglect refers to a response problem that cannot be explained by unawareness or weakness of the limb (Heilman et al., 1993). There may be a failure to move (akinesia), a delay in movement (hypokinesia), movements of decreased amplitude (hypometria), a failure to persist at moving, or a failure to maintain posture (impersistence).

The first type, called "perceptual" neglect, refers to a difficulty in attending to and hence perceiving objects or people on the left side, and has already been discussed under hemispatial neglect. This is primarily considered a problem of input and can be contrasted with a difficulty in moving the responding limb towards the left side of space. This has been termed a problem of "motor intention", or "output" and may involve the non-affected (typically) right hand and the affected (typically) left hand. Such patients may have less difficulty in attending to things on the affected side of space, but show difficulty moving the responding limb into that side of space or in that direction, with their good arm. If we look again at Fig. 1.10a, we can see that John has omitted the left half of the flower. Most therapists and doctors have in the past assumed that this was because the patient has not paid sufficient attention to the left side of the drawing or that he could not adequately represent the left side of the original drawing. However, it is also plausible that he was in fact aware of the left side of the picture, but when asked to copy, had difficulty in moving the right hand into left space when he was drawing. The question remains, whether John's neglect should be diagnosed as a perceptual problem, a motor problem or perhaps a combination of both. Box 1.4 below outlines a recent experiment that helps distinguish the two factors.

The study described in Box 1.4 shows that some patients with neglect have problems attending to things on the left side of space, while others have more difficulty in their intentional or motor directed movements towards the left side of space. There would appear to be two qualitatively different types of motor-related neglect. The first type describes disorders in the preparation to move towards left space and this usually involves the non-paralysed right hand. Three separate features of this type of "pre-motor neglect" have been studied.

BOX 1.4   Perceptual versus pre-motor aspects of neglect

In an attempt to distinguish between perceptual and pre-motor neglect, Halligan and Marshall (1989c), and Bisiach et al. (1990) developed versions of a line bisection task such that one could separate both factors. Others have used more sophisticated experiments using video cameras (Coslett et al., 1990). These tests, in which a subject responds in one half of space to a stimulus presented on the opposite side, helps distinguish attention from intentional deficits in neglect. Such a distinction has obvious implications for rehabilitation. The task employed by Halligan and Marshall (1989c) involved requiring the patient to bisect horizontal lines (ranging in length from 18 to 180mm) displayed on a computer VDU screen. On each trial the "mouse" was used to indicate where the patient considered the midline to be, by moving a marker on the VDU screen. Lines of different length appeared in random order. The experimental set-up for this study is demonstrated in Fig. 1.13.

As can be seen in Fig. 1.13, the congruent condition (Experiment 1) the mouse and cursor always moved in the same direction. In the incongruent condition (Experiment 2) the effects of distinguishing the motor movement from the perceived visual direction allowed the testers to investigate whether motor (intentional) problems were playing a role.

A similar task (involving a string and pulleys) was used by Bisiach in a larger group study. This task, like that due to Halligan and Marshall, comprised two separate conditions. The first (congruent condition) required the patient to indicate the centre of the line by moving a pointer from either end of the line. In the second condition (incongruent) the pointer was indirectly moved by pulling the string to which it was fixed. In this condition deviation of the pointer to the left or right was achieved by a hand movement in the opposite direction. The assumption underlying the task was as follows. In the congruent condition neglect patients would demonstrate the usual rightward deviation. However, in the more interesting incongruent condition, depending on whether the patients neglect was perceptual or pre-motor, it was possible for the bisection to range between two different values. If perceptual factors played a significant role then patients would be expected to make the same error under both conditions. Furthermore, it was found that those patients with pre-motor neglect (deviation of a similar magnitude but in the opposite direction) had strokes which mainly involved the frontal lobes or basal ganglia. Another clever study by Tegnér and Levander (1991), employing mirrors, found a similar distinction.

It is likely that most patients will show a mixture of both types, but it is important clinically to be aware of the possibility that some patients may have more difficulty in moving towards one side of space than in attending to or looking towards that side of space, while for other people the problem might be in attending to one side of space.

A recent study by Marshall and Halligan (1995b) shows another simple way in which it is possible to distinguish between perceptual and perceptual/motor performance. This study (Fig. 3.18) employed a direct comparison of the patient's perceptual judgement of pre-transected lines and that of the patients own perceptual/motor performance. This patient's manual performance was significantly further to the right of non-manual bisection judgement. This experimental set-up allows researchers to distinguish intentional from attentional factors using simple line bisection performance.

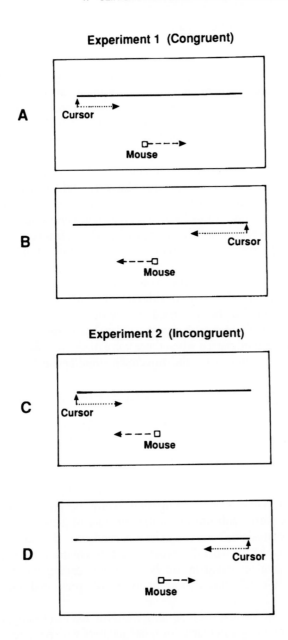

FIG. 1.13 Using a computer mouse, motor and perceptual aspects of line bisection can be distinguished. Reproduced with permission from Halligan, P.W., & Marshall, J.C. (1989c). Perceptual cueing and perceptuo-motor compatibility in visuospatial neglect: A single case study. *Cognitive Neuropsychology*, *6*, 423–435.

(a) *Hemiakinesia* describes a patient's reduced readiness or preparedness to begin to move their right arm into, or towards, left-sided space. Most left neglect patients, and in particular those with lesions involving the posterior cortex, show this directional hypokinesia. This can also refer to eye and head movements. In addition to hemiakinesia, the patient may also show an overall slowness (by comparison with movements into right space) in left space. This has been termed (b) *Bradykinesia*, and refers to the patient's overall slowness in moving the right limb into left-sided space. (c) *Directional Hypometria* refers to a specific deficit in spatial exploration and movement. Patients with this type of pre-motor neglect may show hypometric hand or eye movements towards the neglected side. Although Veronica (Case 4) could verbally indicate the number of playing cards spread out in front of her (six), when requested she could only pick up those cards located on her right-hand side.

"*Motor neglect*" is considered qualitatively distinct from the above difficulties and usually refers to the non use of the affected but nevertheless non-hemiplegic hand or leg. Motor neglect describes the lack of spontaneous use or movement of this affected arm or leg in the absence of severe paralysis. Motor extinction is rarely reported, although this may simply be due to the fact that little research has been carried out. Valenstein and Heilman (1981) reported one case of a man with a right caudate haemorrhage whose left hand movements were unimpaired when these were made in isolation, but became slower when both hands made the movement simultaneously.

NEGLECT DYSLEXIA AND NEGLECT DYSGRAPHIA

Veronica (Case 4) does not show all the problems found in the other three cases. Her main difficulties are restricted to reading and writing. Although she appears able to read some words on the page when they are pointed out to her, she commonly misreads or omits the left side of single words and sentences. She begins each line of text in the middle, reading to the end, then jumps to the middle of the next line. When reading single words, her errors typically involve the removal or partial substitution of the left sides of the word. This has been termed "neglect dyslexia" and can exist independently of other forms of visual neglect. Consequently, specific types of treatment may be needed. Some patients with neglect dyslexia are better when reading words rather than non-words. Table 1.2 shows some of the words presented, along with her responses.

As she is not aware that she is reading words or text incorrectly, this can lead to serious problems, particularly for those patients who have recovered from other physical problems that follow stroke, such as paralysis. It is important to remember that anxiety and/or fatigue can often produce neglect in patients who appear otherwise to have recovered.

TABLE 1.2
Examples of (left) neglect during single word
reading

Word presented	Patient's pronunciation
Catacomb	comb
Gaoled	oled
Depot	pot
Flask	mask
Cuddle	Riddle
University	versity
Liver	Oliver
nausea	undersea
naive	alive
Slave	Have

When asked to write Veronica tends to compress her text over into the right side of the page and omit or double-up strokes and letters. Woodrow Wilson, the American president, also showed neglect dysgraphia after his stroke; his wife had to read most of his personal correspondence to check, and where necessary, correct left-sided omissions. Box 1.5 describes some of the dramatic effects that neglect had on Wilson's recovery.

BOX 1.5   The neglect of Woodrow Wilson

After his stroke in October 1919, the American President, Woodrow Wilson, showed several features of neglect in association with left-sided paralysis that were not at the time recognised as neglect (Weinstein, 1981). Wilson had suffered from progressive cerebral vascular disease throughout most of his life. His wife often had to correct his personal correspondence; he often omitted letters or words located on the left side of the page. Although the President's staff were not necessarily aware of the condition, they were nevertheless very aware of the possible ramifications, particularly for a person holding such high office. This can be gleaned from the fact that in order to avert potential diplomatic incidents where it was possible that the president might ignore (neglect) important visiting foreign dignitaries on the affected side, his aides saw to it that all his guests were ushered to the president's right side. One other outstanding feature of his behaviour was his apparent denial of the physical effects of the stroke (anosognosia). Indeed, Weinstein (1981) suggests that the extent of this anosognosia can be judged from the fact that Wilson attempted to seek a third term of office as president after his second stroke!

NEGLECT OF MENTAL IMAGES

Heilman's classification of neglect phenomenon does not include an important aspect of neglect that was clearly demonstrated by Bisiach and Luzzatti (1978). This clever study showed that neglect could affect mental representations of imagined scenes as well as visual or sensory information. Two of Bisiach's neglect patients, familiar with the Piazza del Duomo in Milan (Fig. 1.14a) were asked while in his office to describe as fully as possible using their imagination, the main square from the two main opposing vantage points. When imagining the cathedral from across the square, these patients mainly reported those landmarks that were located on the right of the real square. They showed a similar omission for left-sided details when subsequently asked to imagine the square from the opposite perspective. In other words, in describing right-sided details in the second perspective, these patients reported previously neglected landmarks! Similar examples have been reported for the Place Neuve in Geneva and for the Place de la Concorde in Paris. Bisiach and Luzzatti (1978) suggested that in neglect, some form of internal picture-like representation of space has become damaged or skewed. They compared it to being "like a sundial" which if destroyed in one quadrant can no longer represent the corresponding arc of time, while regularly functioning for the remainder. Since this original study, different examples of this type of neglect have been reported (Guariglia, Padovani, Pantano, & Pizzamiglio, 1993; Beschin, Cocchini, Della Sala, & Logie, 1997). Another example can be seen in Fig. 1.14b, where a patient with left neglect is asked to describe the states of the US from the perspective of an imaginary flight from east to west. Note how only the states to the north (i.e. on the imagined right) are reported.

Box 1.6 describes several examples where neglect also affected a patient's dreams and hallucinations.

SPATIAL DIMENSIONS OF NEGLECT

Neglect may impair several different spatial domains, including personal body space, peripersonal space (space within reaching or grasping), extrapersonal space (stimuli beyond reaching space), and representational or imaginal space (Rizzolatti & Gallese, 1988; Guariglia et al., 1993; Halligan & Marshall, 1991b). The four cases already described show that there can be differences between neglect involving the body or personal space and reaching space or peripersonal space. There is, however, a further distinction between the space near the body, which is reaching distance, and more distant far space within which we navigate when we walk. We now describe some of the main types of spatial neglect seen after brain damage involving selective areas of space.

(a)

(b)

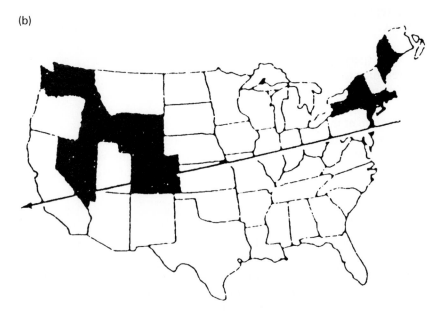

FIG. 1.14 (a)   The famous example of neglect involving mental images: The Milan Square, Italy. (b)   Neglect of some states of the USA during an imagined flight from east to west in a patient with neglect (see direction of arrow). Reprinted with permission of the authors and Oxford University Press from Barbut, D., and Gazzaniga, M. (1987). Disturbances in conceptual space involving language and speech. *Brain*, *110*, 1492.

BOX 1.6   Neglect of dreams and hallucinations

What happens when people with neglect dream? Do such patients with left neglect only "dream" the right side of an image? It seems as if this might be the case. An ingenious study by Doricchi et al. (1991) studied the eye movements which occur when people usually dream. What emerged from their study was that neglect patients made almost all their eye movements to the *right* side, and seldom moved their eyes to the left, suggesting that they showed a similar pattern of eye movements when they were asleep as when they were awake!

Neglect has also been shown to affect patients' reports of their hallucinations. In several cases after unilateral right brain damage, hallucinations have been reported which were confined solely to the right side. Mesulam (1981) described how a chronic alcoholic experienced right-sided hallucinations during a delirium tremens attack several days after suffering a stroke involving the posterior right hemisphere. Similarly, a patient reported by Chamorro et al. (1990) suffered a subcortical infarct and described hallucinations of flying birds located only on the right side of the ward. This patient denied seeing persons or animals in the left side of space.

The representation of space in the brain appears to be designed such that different areas have responsibility for different types of space, namely:

1. body (personal) space;
2. reaching (peripersonal) space;
3. far space (extrapersonal) space.

A diagram of these areas is shown in Fig. 1.15.

The work of Brouchon, Joanette, and Sampson (1985) showed that the area of space we intend to use in a motor movement, e.g. reaching, pointing, writing, or throwing, can strongly influence the choice and extent of visual or perceptual cues used.

Neglect of personal space

In contrast to John (Case 1, pp. 4–6), Rachel (Case 2, pp. 6–7) tends to ignore the left side of her body more. Her left foot regularly becomes entangled beneath the wheelchair plate; her glasses don't catch behind her ear on the left side. She does not put make-up on the left side of her face, and her hair on the left is not tidied. She can, however, attend to most objects in reaching space. Her type of neglect is commonly described as "personal neglect", i.e. a neglect of the left side of her body. Although such patients often show peripersonal neglect, this is not necessarily the case. These two types of neglect probably reflect damage to different parts of the brain, and may require different forms of assessment and treatment.

FIG. 1.15   Different spatial domains that can be neglected independently: Personal, reaching, and far space.

Neglect of peripersonal space

In Case 1, John had most trouble in doing things within "reaching space" surrounding his body. For instance, he could not find his glasses when they were located on the bed or table to his left, and he often banged the left side of his wheelchair into doorways. This form of neglect is by far the most commonly observed and can be readily seen by watching the patient's behaviour on the ward.

Most formal tests of neglect are actually tests of this form of peripersonal neglect, i.e. they are carried out within the patient's normal reaching space. A good example of peripersonal neglect remains that of drawing, as can be seen in Fig. 1.16.

Neglect of extra-personal space

Many patients with peripersonal neglect also show evidence of neglect of extrapersonal or far space; that is in space beyond normal reaching. When asked to describe the contents of their hospital ward, hospital room, or a view of a garden in front of them, some patients describe only features and objects located on their right side. In Box 1.7 there is a description of one study showing evidence for a striking difference between near and far space.

FIG. 1.16   A nice illustration of peripersonal neglect in a drawing of a parrot. Reproduced with permission of The British Psychological Society, from Halligan, P.W. (1995). Drawing attention to neglect: *The Psychologist, 8,* 257–264

BOX 1.7   Neglect for near but not far space

Bill, a 57-year-old mechanic, suffered a large right hemisphere stroke and left-sided neglect. On all the usual clinical tests of visual neglect he showed severe visual neglect. Since there are no formal standardised tests for far or extrapersonal neglect, it was assumed that Bill would show similar problems in far space. However, in the course of answering several questions regarding those aspects of his everyday life that he would most wish to return to, Bill expressed a keen desire to play darts again at his local public house. A good darts player, he had competed and done well in several local tournaments. When given the opportunity to play darts, Bill appeared more than able to direct darts to the intended location irrespective of the side of the board. In an effort to examine what appeared to be a remarkably preserved ability in dart throwing, despite severe visual neglect on all peripersonal clinical tests, a brief experiment was carried out. In order to compare Bill's performance in near and far space using this test, it was necessary to control for the viewing distance. Consequently, in the far space condition, the line lengths used appeared (on the patient's retina) the same as those seen in near space. Using a large board, Bill was asked to divide (bisect) lines into equal halves using a light pen. There were two main conditions and the results are discussed in more detail in Chapter 4. The first condition required Bill to bisect six different lines in peripersonal space. The second involved bisecting six different lines in far space using the light pen. The far space distance used was approximately 244 cm (8 ft). As can be seen from Fig. 1.17, the results of these experiments showed that Bill was much more accurate at bisecting lines in far space than in near space. Furthermore, Bill was also much more accurate at estimating the middle of lines when throwing darts than when bisecting lines in near space! (Halligan & Marshall, 1991b).

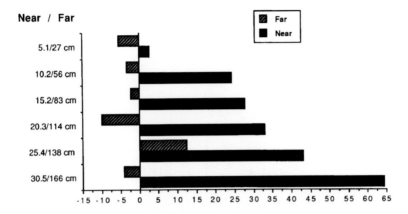

FIG. 1.17   A comparison of neglect for near and far space on line bisection.

Taken collectively, these findings confirm the existence of different areas of space—personal, reaching, and far space. In normals, these spatial circuits no doubt interact interchangeably, in a coordinated way. However, following particular types of damage to the brain, it is possible to find people who are damaged in their attention to just one area of space (Halligan and Marshall, 1991b; Vuilleumier et al., 1998).

WHAT IS NEGLECT "LEFT" OF?

Because unilateral spatial neglect is typically observed under conditions where movements of the eyes and head are permitted, early accounts of neglect tended to assume that the term "left" referred to left of patient's midline or mid-sagittal plane. However, it is probably more accurate to consider a gradient in spatial locations from left to right (Marshall & Halligan, 1989a, Kinsbourne, 1993). The more a stimulus is located to the left, the more frequently it is neglected. There is no constant boundary between the neglected and non-neglected spaces for many patients.

More recent research, however, suggests that the presentation of neglect may nevertheless involve several different frames of reference, including retinal, head, trunk, gravitational, object-centred, and object-based coordinate systems (Halligan and Marshall, 1993b). The body midline is probably one of the most important frames of reference we use. Figure 1.18 shows the consistent effect of neglect of the left side of an object when determined by the patient's body midline.

If a patient attends to the whole table, then he or she may miss most objects located on the left side of the table. On the other hand, if they attend to the

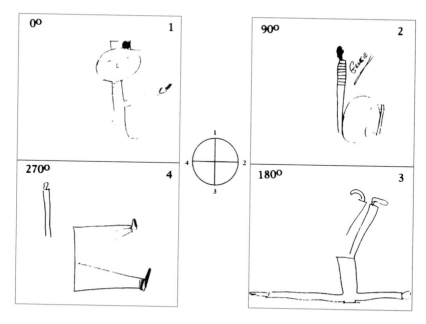

FIG. 1.18   Copies of a simple drawing of a man rotated through 360°: Neglect can be seen to depend on the orientation of the drawing of the man with respect to the patient's midline.

different items on the table, such as the plates, cutlery, etc., they may omit food on the left side of the plate, despite apparently noticing and picking up a fork on the left of the plate on which the food was located.

If what determines the location of neglect is defined solely with respect to the middle of the body, then one should not find patients who neglect the left sides of objects in both right and left space. For instance, when reading the page of a newspaper located to the right of the midline, patients should not miss things on the left side of this right-sided page—if the midline of their body is the sole frame of reference with which neglect is defined. In fact, it is possible to find neglect of the left side of objects, such as the newspaper page, located well over on the right side of space. The reason for this is that the brain damage which gives rise to neglect may impair several different frames of reference or areas of space responsible for designating the relative location of objects in space. It is possible to find neglect of the left side of objects, even when there is no neglect of other objects further to the left in space.

Figure 1.19 shows an example of Rachel's copy of a stimulus figure (see Case 2, pp. 6–7). What is interesting about this drawing is that she clearly is not just missing out the left side of the overall scene, but appears to have missed the

FIG. 1.19   "Object-based" neglect in the case of a copy of a boy and girl.

respective left sides of several of the objects present. For instance, she copies the right side of the boy on the left side of the picture, but misses the left side of the girl further over on the right side. This has been described as a type of "object-based neglect" (Driver & Halligan, 1991). In Fig. 1.19, 'left' applies to the left side of the particular object Rachel happens to be attending to at the time. When her attention is focused on the boy or girl, then she neglects the respective left side of it. These observations are consistent with the position that neglect may involve the left half of information no matter where it appears in the patient's visual field.

OVERVIEW

Collectively, these clinical and experimental findings suggest that neglect, far from being a simple problem of looking to one side, comprises a set of different conditions whose clinical expression depends on damage to several systems involving perceptual and pre-motor processing of spatial information. As we saw from the four cases presented in this chapter, neglect can influence almost every aspect of daily living, from eating and dressing to navigation and pursuing leisure pursuits. Box 1.8 shows how neglect can even interfere with a game of chess.

By studying patients with neglect, we can learn much about the elusive function of attentional and spatial mechanisms and the kinds of information

BOX 1.8   Visual neglect in a chess player

Cherington (1974) reported the effect of neglect on a chess game in a patient after a right parietal lobe stroke. The 52-year-old man who had played chess for most of his life and was considered a good player, began the game with Cherington 4 days before his discharge and 1 month after his stroke. At the time of the game he was alert; however, the manner in which he played showed how his game had suffered as a direct consequence of his neglect of pieces on the left side of the chess board. Despite knowing all the pieces and their moves, the patient demonstrated rather passive defence moves that also affected the right side of the board. When simultaneously confronted with a pawn gambit in the middle of the board and an attack on his queen on his left, he appeared inattentive for the unprotected queen and only recognised his mistaken move (with a groan!) when his queen was captured. Cherington points out that although the patient's spatial perception for "contemplated" moves on the chess board were clearly affected by neglect; the patient could nevertheless recognise accomplished moves on the left side and had "no difficulty in expressing his thoughts about those moves".

processing that can take place with and without conscious awareness (Halligan & Marshall, 1998). The study of patients with neglect has contributed to our knowledge about how different kinds of visual processing can occur at the pre-attentional levels and how information which exists outside conscious awareness may act to influence behaviour. The fact that previous accounts tended to group many of these different aspects under the same clinical label does not do justice to the growing evidence which argues against a unitary coherent syndrome (Halligan & Marshall, 1994d; Robertson & Marshall, 1993; Stone, Halligan, Marshall, & Greenwood, 1998). In the next chapter, we will consider some of the disorders closely associated with neglect.

CHAPTER TWO

Clinical issues for the diagnosis and interpretation of neglect

Although neglect is considered to be a disorder of attention, it is important to be aware of the range of associated perceptual and sensory/motor factors that also influence the way in which the clinical condition manifests itself. As a disorder of attention, neglect can be difficult to disentangle from more basic sensory and motor loss, both in the acute and chronic stages following brain damage (Sterzi et al., 1993). For these reasons, and also because several different factors can contribute to the final clinical presentation of neglect, the clinician diagnosing neglect needs to consider the role of (1) primary sensory/motor loss and (2) non-lateralised attentional processes. These will be considered in more detail in this chapter.

DISORDERS OF PRIMARY SENSORY FUNCTIONING

After hemispheric brain damage, most patients with neglect show impairments of motor, visual, and sensory functions. A study of 36 right brain damaged patients with visual neglect (Hier, Mondlock, & Caplan, 1983a, b) showed the extent of association with other perceptual and motor deficits. A summary of these is shown in Fig. 2.1. From Fig. 2.1, it can be seen that many right brain damaged patients with neglect show problems with face recognition, construction, extinction, arm and leg paralysis, dressing apraxia and visual field deficits. This is not altogether surprising as damage after stroke in particular, tends to involve many areas of the affected hemisphere.

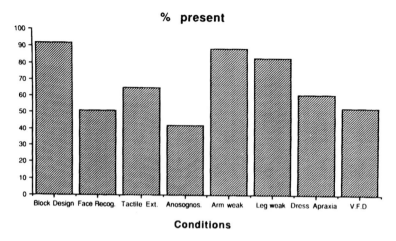

FIG. 2.1   Frequency of perceptual and motor problems in a sample of patients with visual neglect (adapted from Hier et al., 1983).

Several studies in the past have suggested that the observed neglect behaviour might be explained in terms of a loss of visual information from the left side of space (Battersby, Bender, Pollack, & Kahn, 1956). On first consideration, such an explanation appears intuitively plausible since many patients with neglect (as we can see from Fig. 2.1) also have sensory loss involving their visual field deficit. However, the association of visual deficit may arise from the location of the responsible brain damage—a large middle cerebral artery lesions. As the main cause of unilateral neglect, strokes frequently damage the visual fibres connecting the retina and visual cortex and the sensory/motor fibres between the limbs and the somatosensory motor cortex.

VISUAL FIELD DEFICITS

Normal visual fields provide over 200° arc of vision. A schematic illustration of the visual fields and the visual pathways involved is presented in Fig. 2.2. It can be seen from this figure that information from the left side of the visual field projects to the right half of each retina, while the information from the right side projects to the left half of each eye. The visual information on the right half of each retina then passes into the right hemisphere of the brain, and the information on the left half of each eye passes into the left hemisphere of the brain.

Many patients with unilateral neglect have visual field deficits. A visual field cut, also referred to as a hemianopia or scotoma, is the result of damage to the sensory pathways which transmit visual information from the retina to

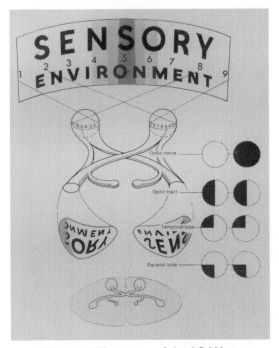

FIG. 2.2   Different types of visual field loss.

those parts within the brain concerned with visual processing. In such patients, visual stimuli falling on the left side of either retina is not fully processed by the brain areas responsible for interpreting incoming signals. Patients with visual field deficits only (without demonstrable signs of visual neglect) are often aware of their visual loss provided that it does not involve central vision. Ishiai, Furukawa, and Tsukagoshi (1987) have shown that such patients often make more saccades to the affected side than normal controls. However, as we will see later on in this chapter, patients with visual field deficits and neglect are not necessarily aware of their sensory loss, and, indeed, many act as if they have a full appreciation of their visual surroundings.

There are several ways to test visual fields (Hensen, 1993). The most common clinical method involves confrontational testing and is illustrated in Fig. 2.3. This method involves the examiner moving a target inward from different locations in the periphery of the subject's visual field. Throughout the clinical examination, the patient is told to report when the target is first detected while they continue to fixate on a central target (usually the examiner's eye or nose). While admittedly crude and somewhat insensitive by comparison with perimeter testing (Trobe, Acosta, Krischer, & Trick, 1981), it does provide the

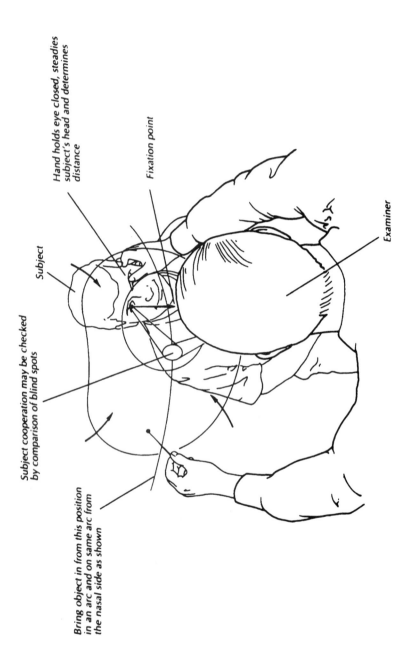

Hand holds eye closed, steadies
subject's head and determines
distance

Fixation point

Subject

Subject cooperation may be checked
by comparison of blind spots

Bring object in from this position
in an arc and on same arc from
the nasal side as shown

Examiner

FIG. 2.3   Clinical testing for visual field defects. Reprinted with permission. From Patten, J. (1996). *Neurological differential diagnosis* (p. 18). Heidelberg: Springer-Verlag.

clinician with an easy method to select patients for more extensive examination. Since the pathways from the retina to the visual cortex are connected in a very precise manner, it is possible using confrontation testing and perimetry to estimate the approximate extent of the visual field deficit.

Field deficits that occur in association with neglect involve damage to the optic tract radiations as they project from the optic chiasm through the temporal, parietal, and occipital lobes of the right hemisphere. Consequently, most visual field deficits after large strokes involve the left half of each eye's visual field (that is, an homonymous hemianopia).

Distinguishing visual neglect from visual field deficits

Studies comparing the eye movements of patients with homonymous hemianopia and unilateral visual neglect, have shown that, in the early stages, both groups may show a similar pattern when say, reading a page of text (Karnath, 1994). Both tend to read from the right, and then make long eye movements back across the page leftwards, but typically fail to reach the left side. Most patients then make a series of small step-like compensatory eye movements towards the left, until they find a meaningful or plausible place to begin reading. Depending on the content and difficulty of the text, this may or may not be the actual left side of the page.

Patients with homonymous hemianopia often report that they bump into people or things on the street, and that they may at times fail to notice something or someone on the left side, located in their blind field. Box 2.1 describes a humorous incident following a visual field deficit.

Distinguishing neglect from hemianopia is not as straightforward as it would at first appear; both assessments ultimately rely on the patient's ability to report or respond to specific targets located on the affected side. The real problem, however, occurs when one attempts to reconcile what appears to be the incongruous results of two types of testing; one in which a patient shows neglect but not a visual field deficit and vice versa. Since neglect implies a failure to attend to stimuli in the left field (e.g. a failure to detect targets on the left side of a cancellation or copying task), how is it possible for the same patient to reliably indicate stimuli located in the same visual field when tested on confrontational visual field testing?

One potential way of distinguishing between a lesion of the visual pathways and one that produces neglect is to take advantage of the fact that visual fields loss is considered to be purely retinopic, whereas neglect has been traditionally defined in terms of the patient's midsaggital plane. If a patient with left-sided neglect is instructed to attend to his/her right, both visual fields now fall within the intact hemispace. Using standard confrontational testing techniques, but employing different lateralised positions, Nadeau and Heilman (1991) reported

Box 2.1   Benign consequences of a visual field deficit

As a direct result of a mild stroke which damaged part of his right occipital cortex two weeks before, Bryan Kolb (one of the co-authors of *Fundamentals of Human Neuropsychology*, 1993) suffered a field deficit which affected his left upper visual field. Two weeks after his stroke, Kolb was looking for Ian Whishaw (the co-author) in the psychology department as they were scheduled to go to a meeting. Kolb looked into a large room in the department where he expected to see Ian. On seeing nobody, he concluded that Ian had left without him. In fact, Whishaw was on the telephone in the room but was seated to the left of Kolb's field of vision. For his own part, Whishaw believed that Kolb, having seen him on the 'phone, was waiting for him elsewhere. What had happened, however, is that because Whishaw had fallen within Kolb's scotoma, he could not see him in the room when he had first looked. When they eventually met up, considerable confusion followed as each had attributed accounts on the basis of what they did see at the time. (Adapted from Kolb & Whishaw, 1993.)

a patient (without evidence of visual neglect) who showed a "gaze-dependent hemianopia"; when the patient directed his gaze 30° to the right (such that the left retinopic field was now in right hemispace) he showed a marked improvement in movement detection, object naming, shape identification, and colour naming by comparison with the standard condition. The authors indicate that it is possible that the standard confrontation condition results in this case represent more than just primary visual dysfunction, and that the gaze direction effects result from the influence of attentional or intentional factors. This speculation finds support in an earlier study by Kooistra and Heilman (1989). Using confrontation assessment, Kooistra and Heilman described a patient with a right thalamic and temporo-occipital lesion who appeared to have a left visual field defect. The same patient also showed neglect on many standard tasks such as line cancellation and line bisection. Kooistra and Heilman were curious to see whether the side of hemispace where the confrontation testing took place could effect the response. When the patient's eyes were directed either straight ahead (as in the traditional confrontation testing) or 30° towards the left, the patient failed to report stimuli presented in the relative left visual field. However, when her eyes were directed 30° towards right hemispace the visual field defect appeared to resolve suggesting that the patient had visual neglect which, upon conventional confrontation testing, had masqueraded as a visual field defect. The results of the patient are summarised in Fig. 2.4.

The findings of Kooistra and Heilman (1989) suggest that the results of visual field testing using perimetry or confrontation may have been confounded with visual neglect. Box 2.2 illustrates the complexity of some of the issues involved in distinguishing neglect from a visual field deficit.

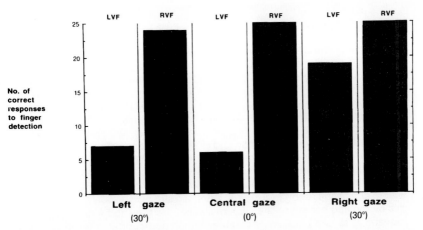

FIG. 2.4 Performance of a patient with an apparent hemianopia which varied depending on which way his eyes were looking. When gazing centrally, detections in the left visual field (LVF) were less than in the right (RVF). This was also the case when gazing to the left. With right gaze, on the other hand, the number of left-sided detections increased dramatically: in other words, an attentional disorder was masquerading as a peripheral visual disorder (adapted from Kooistra and Heilman, 1989).

Although the presence of a visual field deficit may indeed contribute to impaired processing in the acute stage, there is considerable evidence to suggest that it is neither necessary nor sufficient *alone* to produce problems in free vision. Even more convincing is the fact that both conditions have been shown to double dissociate (Halligan, Marshall, & Wade, 1990b); that is, there are patients with right brain damage who show visual neglect but not a visual field deficit and there are also patients who show a visual field deficit without neglect. Furthermore, eye movement recordings have clearly shown that hemianopic patients employ a series of stepwise saccadic eye movements which allow them to find and fixate objects initially located in the blind hemifield.

Even in the absence of attentional factors, it is not clear how a primary visual field deficit could produce florid neglect behaviours. The presence of a primary sensory loss per se does not prevent the patient (in free vision) from moving their eyes to search for the incomplete end of a word, line, or object that they should, presumably, be aware of as missing and without which the word, sentence, or object would clearly not make sense. Other differences between neglect and visual field defects that have been pointed out include differences in the sites of the lesions and recovery rates.

Further distinguishing features include the fact that unilateral neglect will often present in other modalities and does not depend on the patient actually looking at something. For instance, in some cases indicated in Chapter 1

Box 2.2   When is a visual field not a visual field ?

Robin Walker and his colleagues in Durham, UK, studied a woman who had severe left-sided neglect and who had been diagnosed by her neuro-ophthalmologist as suffering from a left homonymous hemianopia, using standard perimetry: her visual fields chart looked very similar to the one in Fig. 1.5 in Chapter 1. Walker and his colleagues also found that the woman did not report things on the left side of a computer screen when they tested her, apparently confirming the presence of a homonymous hemianopia. In both these procedures, however, the woman had to stare at a central fixation point while waiting to detect stimuli on either side. Ingeniously, Walker "switched off" the central fixation point a very short time (roughly a sixth of a second) before presenting the test stimuli on the left side. When this was done, the woman was able to detect and report more of the left-sided stimuli: she couldn't have done this by moving her eyes, as a sixth of a second is too short a time for an eye movement to take place. Why had the woman not reported the stimuli when there was a central fixation point? This was because the testing procedure of central fixation used in visual field testing was in itself inadvertently attracting attention. Consequently, cueing the patient's attention to a central point produced an extinction of the left-sided event. In this case the visual field deficit was more apparent than real. The visual field cut, given the traditional procedures used for testing for it, hid the fact that the real underlying deficit was one of attention—namely extinction (see Chapter 1). The study by Walker et al. (1991) indicates that the procedural aspects (of maintaining central fixation) in perimetry or confrontation testing were in themselves contributing to attentional-like deficits in visual field testing.

neglect can occur when recalling features from mental images. When asked to imagine walking down the local high street, patients tend to describe shops and buildings on the right, but not on the left. In other cases, patients may fail to wash or dress the left side of their body, or explore left-sided space, even with their eyes closed. Clearly these problems cannot be attributed to a failure to "see" the left side. That is, the fact that patients with brain damage cannot "see" to their left after stroke does not in itself easily explain the range of neglect behaviour observed.

Furthermore, patients with neglect behaviours may show extinction (see Chapter 1) in modalities other than the visual one. They may, for instance, respond to a single sound presented to their left ear, but fail to detect a left sound when presented in combination with a right one. Similarly, they may detect a touch on the left arm, but fail to detect a left touch when there is a simultaneous right one. While the existence of such auditory or tactile extinction does not definitely prove that omissions on the left side are caused by unilateral neglect rather than homonymous hemianopia, they provide additional evidence in the context of other clinical information.

There is also considerable evidence that many patients with homonymous hemianopia learn over time to develop a consistent set of compensatory eye and head movements directed over to the affected side (Ishiai et al., 1987; Meienberg, Harrer, and Wehren 1981). This is shown in a case of a copying task reported by Meienberg et al. (1986) (Fig. 2.5).

It is possible using eye movement recordings to distinguish between the two conditions; some of these differences are summarised in Table 2.1. In neglect, there is the additional deficit of not knowing where and how far to look (Meienberg, 1983). Given awareness of their tendency to miss things on the left side, many patients with visual field deficits spontaneously learn to make frequent "checks" in the form of fast eye movements over to the left side, so that anything happening on the left side, not automatically detected, can be easily seen by the intact right visual field. Indeed, some patients with a visual field

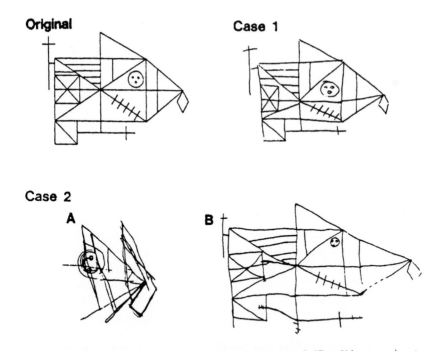

FIG. 2.5 Comparison of figure copying in a patient with hemianopia (Case 1) in comparison to a case with both hemianopia and neglect (Case 2). Case 1 missed no details, even in the acute stage following the lesion. Case 2, on the other hand, did not show an appropriate copy until 7 months later, despite still having a hemianopia (Meienberg et al., 1986). Reproduced with permission of Springer-Verlag from Meienberg, O., Harrer, M., and Wehren, C. (1986). Oculographic diagnosis of hemineglect in patients with homonymous hemianopia. *Journal of Neurology, 233*, 97–101.

Table 2.1

Behavioural characteristics of people with hemianopia in comparison to the behaviour of people with unilateral neglect (Meienberg et al., 1986).

	Hemianopia	Visual neglect
Saccades	Many spontaneous searching saccades across midline	Few or any searching saccades across midline
	Immediate reaction with searching saccades after disappearance of fixated target	Little or no reaction after disappearance of fixated target
	Learns to predict target position after a few successful searching movements	No prediction of target location when removed from fixation
	Increase of searching saccade size with time	Small size of saccades persists
Reading	Initially some difficulty finding the left edge of the line—later overshooting compensation.	Missing parts of words and sentences beginning on the left side
Pursuit movement	Pursuit of target to its extreme position even on the hemianopic side	Insufficient pursuit of target towards hemineglect side

deficit affecting the left side are *faster* than normals in detecting stimuli on the left side of space on certain tasks (Ishiai et al., 1987). However, if one compares patients with unilateral neglect who have no visual field defects with those who have, one finds no significant difference in the severity of unilateral neglect on visual tasks (Halligan, et al., 1990b).

Although patients with visual field deficits are often able to compensate for this impairment, the current regulations from the Driver and Vehicle Licensing Agency (DVLA) in the UK preclude return to driving if a patient has a complete lower quadrant defect or homonymous hemianopia. Details of medical aspects of fitness to drive are available from the Medical Commission on Accident Prevention. Further details as to how visual field defects affect driving are described in Box 2.3. Interestingly, given that neglect is often more debilitating and potentially dangerous than visual field defects, the current DVLA guidelines (March 1996) do not specifically mention neglect as a reason for not being able to drive.

Reference to "neglect" is only briefly made under cognitive disorders after stroke. They suggest that an in-car assessment, conducted by a qualified driving instructor on the road, is sufficient to ensure that visual inattention should not cause the patient to be a source of danger. No details as to how neglect behaviours are evaluated during the assessment are provided. Although the in-car assessments are no doubt crucial, as they provide information on the

Box 2.3   Neglect and driving

An adequate field of vision is necessary for driving and the recent European Union directive and the advice from the Royal College of Ophthalmologists, defines the minimal field of vision for safe driving as 120°. There is some evidence that drivers with visual fields less than 120° are more prone to accidents, particularly on the side of the visual loss. Johnson and Keltner (1983) indicated that patients with significant field loss had twice the average number of road traffic accidents. Until recently, people who had suffered strokes were not normally re-issued with a licence until a year after the stroke. The decision as to whether a stroke victim is granted a licence is primarily made on medical grounds. Until recently, there has been little consideration given to the effect of stroke on higher level, perceptual, and spatial disorders. For most stroke patients, cars can be adapted to suit their physical requirements. Without assessment and rehabilitation such adaptions are of little use when considering perceptual and spatial deficits. In order to negotiate a car on the road safely, a driver needs to process new visual information continually and make appropriate decisions. The failure to notice relevant cues can lead to potentially dangerous situations, e.g. failure to detect a stop sign on the left at a busy junction, driving too close to the kerb or other parked cars, failing to notice pedestrians or cars approaching from the left. The ability to appreciate one's spatial environment is crucial for general car positioning, overtaking, parking, and reversing. Sivak et al. (1981) showed that driving performance was directly related to the degree of perceptive impairment in a group of 31 patients. Case reports which show that visual field deficits in association with neglect behaviours can be potentially dangerous for driver and pedestrians have been described. One striking report described by Lachenmayr and Vivell (1993) concerned a 53-year-old man who demonstrated a left homonymous hemianopia after a grenade injury. Not willing to accept the fact that this prevented him from driving, he went to great extents to compensate for his loss of vision by using "mirror spectacles" and positioning a marker line on the windshield of his car. When driving, this patient attempted to constantly fixate to the left of the line. The so-called "mirror spectacles", because they projected part of the lost visual field into the normal half, produced on Goldman perimetry fairly useful visual fields. Despite making spatial orientation in the defective hemifield possible, the effect, however, did not provide for safe driving as the correlation with spatial objects is lost; the normal hemifield continues to image objects of the normal field as well as objects of the opposite mirror field. Since the patient could satisfy the criteria of Goldman perimetry using the "mirror spectacles", he was permitted to drive. Only after a prolonged court case, which resulted from several accidents including one in which a pedestrian was killed, was it possible to officially revoke this driver's licence.

patient's actual performance rather than extrapolations from clinical tests, there are occasions (Simms, 1985) when the driving test fails to support clinical results. This anomaly may be explained in terms of the patient's over-familiarisation with the driving task together with the fact that the driving assessment may elicit a patient's potentially best performance.

The effect of somatosensory loss

Similar problems with the differential diagnosis of neglect occur in the somato-sensory modality. If a patient persistently fails to care for or use their hemiplegic left arm or leg, or if a patient fails to dress properly on the left side of the body, can this not be simply explained in terms of the absence or impair-ment of sensory input from that side of the body? How do we know that Rachel, in Chapter 1, (pp. 6–7), was not similarly impaired due to a simple loss of somatosensory information from her hemiplegic side?

As with the visual modality, the best way of distinguishing neglect from somatosensory loss is to observe the difference when attention is drawn to or away from the impaired side. If the patient can detect single stimuli located on the left side of the body (say the hand, arm, leg, or cheek), but only notice a right-sided stimuli when both sides are stimulated, then clearly an attentional account is more likely. This method, however, does not help to distinguish what may be going on when the patient fails to detect single stimuli on the left side. In such cases it may be difficult to distinguish between the effects of an attentional or basic sensory loss. Vallar et al. (1991) showed that neglect phenomena are possible even in those patients who showed otherwise normal physiological processing of the undetected stimuli on the affected side. That an attentional problem can in some cases underlie what appears to be a sensory loss is shown by the work of Vallar and his colleagues in Milan, Italy, which is described in more detail in Box 2.4.

Clinically, however, it is not possible or desirable to carry out the procedures of caloric stimulation described in Box 2.4; the important diagnostic question remains how to distinguish basic sensory loss from attention-based behaviours. This may not be as much of a problem as it seems, however, as loss of sensation

Box 2.4   Producing feeling in the sensory impaired arm

It has been known for many years that stimulation of the vestibular system of the brain by a "caloric stimulation" can produce a dramatic but short-lived improvement in neglect (see Chapter 6). Caloric stimulation, which involves the radical procedure of syringing iced water into the patients' ears, has the affect of activating both the vestibular system and some of the related cortical and subcortical areas affected by the brain damage. Vallar et al. (1990) has also shown that this procedure could assist sensation, albeit temporarily, in the affected side of the body, suggesting that the original anaesthesia may not have been caused by basic sensory factors, but by attentional ones which could be briefly but strikingly remedied by caloric stimulation.

in itself seldom results in a lack of attention to the affected limb. Many patients often rub their arms, remarking on the lack of sensation: that is, despite the absence of information such patients are clearly aware of the existence of the affected limb. Even if they do not have somatosensory input from the arm, they have the awareness of that side of their body, and a corresponding awareness that a certain input is missing from that region.

The effect of proprioceptive loss

As with visual field defects and somatosensory impairments, loss of proprioceptive information often suggests a basic sensory deficit. However, as with previous disorders, some cases of proprioceptive damage appear to have an attentional basis. Vallar et al. (1993) demonstrated this using a method known as "opto-kinetic stimulation", which involves presenting patients with a moving background, constantly drifting from right to left. This technique stimulates the vestibular system, results "in the eyes been dragged leftward", and is in a way comparable to the effects of caloric stimulation (see Box 2.3). Optokinetic stimulation, like vestibular stimulation, can produce a temporary reduction in neglect. Vallar and colleagues have shown that optokinetic stimulation also improved proprioceptive loss in neglect patients. Patients' left arms were placed in a number of different positions behind a screen, and patients had to judge their relevant position. When they made these judgements while staring at a moving optokinetic inducing background, they were much more accurate. These findings confirm that many apparently basic sensory deficits may actually be caused by neglect-type attentional disorders.

The effect of primary motor loss

Most patients with neglect suffer extensive motor loss which affects their left side. The assumption has been that this hemiplegia largely results from the damage to the basic motor pathways. As with apparently basic sensory disorders, however, there is now evidence that vestibular stimulation can produce a temporary recovery in the previously paralysed or motor weakened side of the body (Rode & Perenin, 1994; Vallar et al., 1990). Such an improvement is not possible if the primary motor tract lesions were solely responsible for the hemiparesis. As with the sensory findings described earlier, this finding suggests that at least some of these problems in neglect patients may be attentional. If further evidence of this can be found in other patients with neglect, then this would clearly have major implications for rehabilitation. Indeed, later in this book (Chapter 5) we discuss motor activation based treatments for neglect.

Evidence regarding attentional problems producing what seem to be purely sensory or motor problems help make sense of the study described in Box 2.5.

The role of "pathological completion"

As we have seen, it is not uncommon for neglect patients to fail to notice the loss of vision or touch on the affected side. Why do patients fail to draw, copy, or write on the left side in free vision? The failure to detect has been interpreted by some researchers as an example of "perceptual completion"—a process not reserved for neurologically impaired patients. All neurologically normal subjects lack phenomenological experience of our naturally occurring blind spot. The blindspot corresponds to the place on the retina where the optic nerve leaves the eyeball. Despite this "hole" in our visual field (which has to be demonstrated in order to become temporarily aware of it), we do not experience a discernible "hole" in our perceptual experience of the world. Some researchers (Gassell & Williams, 1963) consider "pathological completion" to be similar to the process of normal completion. However it is not clear whether the process involved in patients with neglect is really a filling-in process or a failure to be aware of the left side (Walker and Mattingley, 1997).

Halligan and Marshall (1994a) reported visual completion in a patient with severe neglect. An example of this patient's performance is shown in Fig. 2.6. When presented with a full butterfly to copy, the patient drew the body and right wing but nevertheless reported upon questioning and in free vision that the copied butterfly was indeed a full butterfly. Consequently in these and other more functional examples (and unless specifically cued to the left side), it would appear that some patients with left neglect behave as if the "whole" objects or scenes have been seen or recognised.

Box 2.5 "Hidden" neglect

Sterzi et al., (1993) studied more than 100 stroke patients with right brain damage, and compared them with a similar number who had left brain damage. Surprisingly, the right brain damaged group showed more visual field defects, motor loss, and proprioceptive loss than the left brain damaged group. At first glance this is an unlikely finding, as it is generally assumed that basic motor and sensory pathways are symmetrically distributed in the two hemispheres. Another way of putting this is to say that there is no known anatomical or physiological reason why one would expect damage to one side of the brain to produce more basic sensory or motor loss than the other. The answer to this potentially puzzling finding is probably because right brain damage is associated with attentional deficits. Given the possibility of misdiagnosis of neglect in terms of basic deficits, it is not surprising that attentional loss for the affected side has been missed.

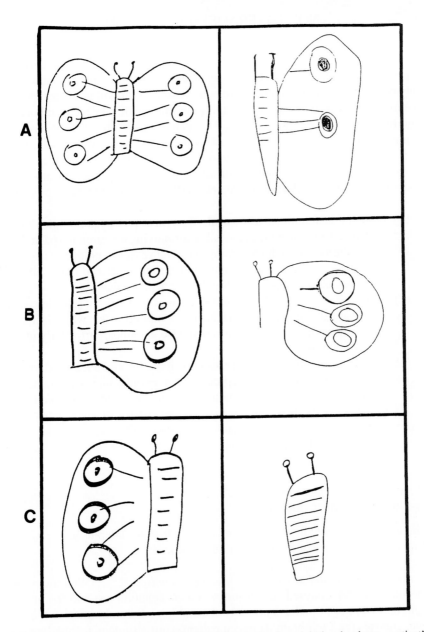

FIG. 2.6 Copies of a butterfly: left-hand column—stimulus; right-hand column—patient's copy. In A, the left wing of the butterfly is missed. In B, the copy is similar to the stimulus. In C, only the body is copied, as the single wing is on the left (neglected) side (Halligan and Marshall, 1994a). Reproduced with permission of Clinica Neurologica from Halligan, P.W., and Marshall, J.C. (1994). Completion in visuospatial neglect: A case study. *Cortex, 30*, 685–694.

NON-LATERALISED ATTENTION

In the previous section, we showed how loss of attention to one side of space—whether due to neglect or extinction—can produce a far greater range of problems than has hitherto been recognised. Attention to space is, however, only one type of attention, and there is no reason to think that other types of attentional loss do not complicate the presentation of neglect in clinically significant ways. Furthermore, as shall be seen in Chapter 6 it may be possible to improve lateralised forms of neglect by using relatively independent, non-lateralised attentional systems. To understand the complexity of attentional factors involved, it is necessary to consider the main types of normal attention systems. The model by Posner and Peterson (1990) involves three components:

(1) Orientation attentional system, also known as the "posterior attentional system". This system is responsible for moving attention in space. It is one of the systems which is compromised in cases of unilateral neglect. This attentional system is located in the inferior parietal lobes, but the thalamus and the superior colliculus are also involved.

(2) Selective attention system. This system is responsible for selecting what is relevant and important, and ignoring or inhibiting that which is irrelevant. This is thought to be based in the frontal lobes, particularly in the anterior cingulate gyrus.

(3) Sustained attention system (also known as the vigilance or alertness system). This system is responsible for maintaining a readiness to respond in the absence of novel or otherwise "attention-grabbing" external events. It is thought to have particularly strong inputs to the orientation or posterior attentional system. The system is strongly lateralised in the right hemisphere, particularly in the right frontal lobe and right parietal lobe.

How non-lateralised attentional systems are impaired after neglect?

There is evidence that neglect is linked to more that just lateralised attentional problems. Four types of evidence will be reviewed:

(a) Evidence of deficits within ipsilesional hemispace.   Weintraub and Mesulam (1989) analysed search times in a cancellation test and found that right brain damaged patients not only showed longer search times on the left than controls (and left brain damaged patients) but also demonstrated longer right search times than left brain damaged patients, for whom this was their impaired side. They attribute this ipsilesional result to the right hemisphere having an attentional role for both sides of space. Damage to the right hemisphere resulted in both bilateral and unilateral attentional deficits, they argued.

Some commentators (Gainotti & Bartolomeo, 1991), have argued that these results are open to an alternative explanation, namely that patients often neglect with respect to some retinotopically based midline, which may not be related to the midline of the entire text. For example, in a densely packed visual task such as that used by Weintraub and Mesulam, what is neglected may relate to a continuously shifting midline within a correspondingly moving narrow attentional field, even when the patient is searching to the right side of the stimulus array. By this argument, omissions on the ipsilesional side may reflect simple lateralised neglect of localised areas of the target array. While this argument is an important one, it is not uncommon to observe left neglect patients who neglect at the very right extremity of the stimulus array.

Robertson (1989) proposed that a non-lateralised attentional deficit was also present in cases of unilateral left visual neglect, and predicted that one result of this would be a significant increase in right-sided omissions when left neglect patients were cued to the left, when compared with controls (in this case by being required to read a simple word under the left stimulus location at the same time as detecting the target stimuli), during the presentation of rapid single or double stimuli. This prediction was substantiated with left cueing, resulting in the equalising of left versus right errors among the left neglect patients. In other words, when the patient's attention was attracted to the right side, they began to show as many errors on the right side as they did on the left, showing many more errors than normal controls.

This finding is also found in clinical attempts to treat the condition. In one patient seen by PWH several years ago, the net effect of 3 weeks systematic left-sided scanning was a reliable reduction of left neglect accompanied by a increase in the neglect of right-sided targets on post-intervention testing.

Other evidence of non-lateralised factors playing a role can be seen in the case of line bisection performance. Marshall and Halligan (1989b) have shown that not only is the displacement of line bisection greater to the right in patients with neglect, but that the standard deviations of those bisection displacements is also much greater than when compared to normals. Unilateral neglect performance was explained in terms of a combination of two distinct impairments. One impairment was the consistent right-to-left approach to an "indifference zone" or approximate area of perceived middle of the line; the second was a greater zone of subjective uncertainty (also known as the *Weber fraction*). In other words, apart from the lateralised deficit, a non-lateralised deficit in perceptual estimation leads to a bigger margin of error in the bisection judgement of neglect subjects.

(b) Evidence for increased neglect with increased demands on attention. Rapcsak and colleagues (1989) examined the degree of left hemi-inattention shown by a group of patients in a simple cancellation task under three conditions. The first required the patient to cancel all targets from a group of simple

stimuli. The second required cancellation of only those from a group of similar stimuli (which differed from the other stimuli by one simple feature) with a "dot" in the top right (or left) hand corner. In the third condition, the stimulus to be cancelled had a dot in the top right (or left) hand corner but, in addition to the foils used in the first condition, there were additional foils which had a dot in the bottom right (or left) hand corner which were also to be ignored. The last condition differed from the other two only in that it required more selective attention from the subject, i.e. the subjects had to select stimuli from among a greater variety of competing choices.

The authors found that the degree of neglect in the third condition was significantly greater than in the other two, suggesting a deterioration in hemi-inattention under greater non-lateralised attentional load. This finding has subsequently been replicated (Kaplan et al., 1991). Robertson and Frasca (1992) also studied the effects of engaging in an attentionally demanding secondary task (counting backwards in 3's from 100) while carrying out a simple visual detection task for briefly presented stimuli. In two out of four patients with left neglect, the latency of response for left stimuli significantly lengthened in comparison to that for right stimuli.

(c) Evidence for the influence of degree of arousal upon neglect.   Fleet and Heilman (1986) compared the performance of neglect patients on the administration of repeated letter cancellation tasks under two conditions—one with feedback of results, one with no feedback. The feedback consisted simply of them being told the number of errors they had made after each cancellation trial. With serial administrations over a short time period, neglect increased in the no-feedback condition, but decreased in the feedback condition. The authors interpret this as being due to improved arousal as a result of feedback of results, producing a reduction in neglect, though of course other interpretations are possible, and the phenomenon cannot unequivocally be attributed to increased arousal (as shall be seen in Chapter 6). However, increasing arousal levels can produce specific improvements in neglect (Robertson et al., 1995).

Robertson, Mattingley, Rorden, and Driver (1998) have shown how neglect can be transiently reduced or even abolished through increasing arousal with nonlateralised auditory tones.

(d) Dysfunctional compensatory scanning procedures.   Box 2.6 gives details of a study which at first glance gives a puzzling result, but with further inspection offers a clue as to the way in which the different attentional systems may interact. The findings described in Box 2.6 may be explained in the following way. Most patients show neglect soon after stroke; however, the vast majority recover from the condition to the same degree within a couple of weeks. Recovery is far greater and faster in left hemisphere lesion patients (Stone et al., 1992). It seems to be the case that (at least for some patients)

Box 2.6   When left goes right?

Figure 2.7 shows the letter cancellation performance of a woman who suffered very clearly defined damage to the right hemisphere of her brain. She showed typical patterns of left motor problems and left neglect on most tests. Figure 2.8, however, shows her copy from memory of a clock face, which is clearly a strange one. On that drawing, all the numbers are drawn on the left-hand side, with apparent neglect of the right. Such paradoxical right-sided omissions in patients with right-sided lesions are not uncommon. From a sample of 90 stroke cases throughout Europe, 17 were identified who showed more neglect of the right than the left on some tests. Possible explanations for these findings can be found in the main text.

recovery can be brought about by patients learning to compensate by scanning their attention towards the left. A study by Goodale, Milner, Jakobson, and Carey, (1990) provides some relevant evidence for this interpretation. They studied a group of nine subjects who had suffered unilateral right hemisphere lesions with a mean of 21 weeks after the onset of the lesion. Many of these patients had previously shown signs of unilateral neglect, but by the time they were tested showed no clinical neglect.

The experiment by Goodale et al. consisted of two tasks, one involving reaching out and touching one of a number of targets presented on a vertical screen in front of the subjects, and the other requiring the subjects to bisect the distance between two specified targets on a screen. The brain damaged patients showed no difference from the controls on their accuracy of touching the targets, whereas they did show a significant tendency to bisect to the right of the true midpoint of the distance between adjacent targets, suggesting the existence of an enduring subclinical manifestation of left unilateral neglect for bisection which was revealed by standard clinical testing. More interesting, however, were the trajectories paths of the hand movements as they reached to the targets. In both the target and the bisection conditions, kinematic analysis of the reaching movements revealed that the patients made a wider right arc into the final target, a pattern not apparent in the controls. While this may be accounted for by ipsilateral weakness, it is more likely that it reflected some spatial bias in attention that, although evident was compensated for in the final movements of the task.

These results suggest that, even after the apparent recovery of neglect, underlying distortions in spatial or attentional mechanisms may still exist. It may be the case that such patients learn to correct for their neglect by self-learnt compensatory strategies. When the patients first made their ballistic trajectories, it appears that they may have done so on the basis of a distorted proprioceptive body-referenced spatial system. This rightward trajectory was

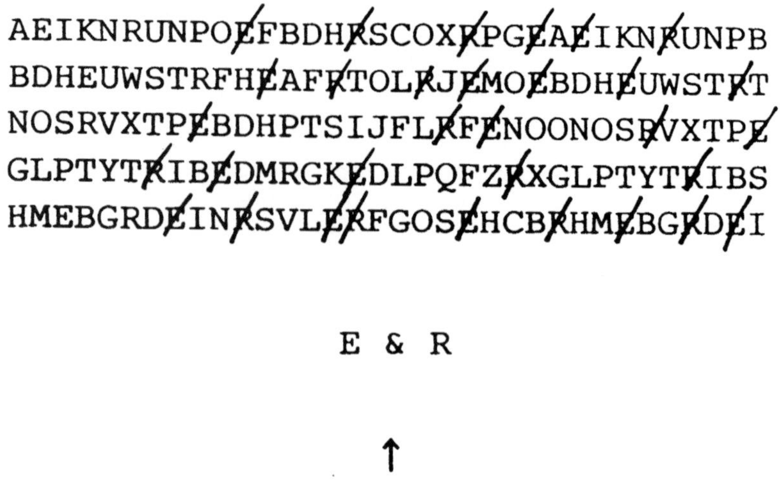

AEIKNRUNPOEFBDHRSCOXRPGEAEIKNRUNPB
BDHEUWSTRFHEAFRTOLRJEMOEBDHEUWSTRT
NOSRVXTPEBDHPTSIJFLRFENOONOSRVXTPE
GLPTYTRIBEDMRGKEDLPQFZRXGLPTYTRIBS
HMEBGRDEINRSVLERFGOSEHCBRHMEBGRDEI

E & R

↑

FIG. 2.7   Letter cancellation showing left-sided omissions consistent with the right hemisphere lesion (Robertson et al., 1994a). Reproduced with permission of Clinica Neurologica from Robertson, I.H., Halligan, P.W., Bergego, C., Hömberg, V., Pizzamiglio, L., Weber, E., and Wilson, B.A. (1994). Right neglect following right hemisphere damage. *Cortex, 30,* 199–214.

FIG. 2.8   Drawing of clock face by a woman who did the test shown in Fig. 2.7. Here the side of neglect is dramatically reversed (Robertson et al., 1994a). Reproduced with permission of Clinica Neurologica from Robertson, I.H., Halligan, P.W., Bergego, C., Hömberg, V., Pizzamiglio, L., Weber, E., and Wilson, B.A. (1994). Right neglect following right hemisphere damage. *Cortex, 30,* 199–214.

then corrected by a compensatory visual feedback system in which subjects spontaneously learned to correct the spatial errors of which they were aware. Alternatively, they may not have been aware of the deficits, and these compensatory visual responses may have been elicited by some kind of conditioning process along the lines of those which have been hypothesised to occur in hemianopics spontaneously learning to compensate for their visual field deficits (mentioned earlier in this chapter). Using results from clinical testing, Campbell and Oxbury (1976) also made such an interpretation assuming that patients had become more proficient on certain tasks following practice.

If it is true that underlying deficits still persist which are hidden by compensatory mechanisms, then it would be possible to elicit the basic deficit by presenting a task which is attentionally demanding or requires a high degree of spatial thought. An example of the former may explain the results of cases reported by Robertson and Frasca (1992), where left–right differences in response latency only emerged during an attentionally demanding secondary task performance. An example of the latter may explain poor performance of Goodale et al.'s subjects on the bisection task compared to the target pointing task.

A second example of the possible existence of a learned compensatory scanning procedure comes from a study by Pierson-Savage et al. (1988). They found that vibrotactile reaction times (tactile stimulation applied to a finger of right hand) in a group of left neglect subjects were significantly longer when the arm was in the left half of space than when in the right half of space. The same subjects were then retested after a period of rehabilitation, and it was found that they were now faster with their arms on the left side of space than on the right. In both this test and the preceding one, they were tested with their eyes open. In the retest condition, however, the authors also tested the subjects on the same task with their eyes closed.

When this happened, the subjects reverted to their old pattern, namely being slower on the right side of space than on the left. What this suggests is that the reversal of the left-sided slowness after rehabilitation was based upon some kind of learned visual scanning response, even though the task itself was a vibrotactile one. When the eyes were closed, this presumably compensatory response was eliminated, and hence the subjects reverted to the persisting and underlying bias towards the right side of space.

In summary, therefore, anomalous "right-sided inattention" may occur in some right brain damaged patients with left neglect when they deploy a compensatory scanning strategy in the context of a persisting non-lateralised attentional deficit. These omissions are more likely to emerge when the task requires scanning of a visual array which consists of a number of different elements, though it can also occur in relatively simple visual arrays such as in the line bisection task or in the drawing from memory tasks. While other explanations can be advanced to explain these results, one possibility is that these are patients who have learned to try to compensate for their neglect by scanning to the left. However, because they have problems with more than one of the attentional systems outlined above, and because their attentional problems are not just confined to one side, but include non-lateralised attentional problems, at times when they do scan to the left, this results in them omitting stimuli to the right-hand side. Clinically, there are examples where the requirement to deal with non-lateralised attentional demands can reveal or worsen existing lateralised forms of neglect. For example, it is commonly observed that fatigue, anxiety, or anger can show up neglect in patients who otherwise appear to have recovered (cf. Box 4.5 in Chapter 4). Furthermore, requiring a "recovered" patient to engage in conversation while walking often provides an illustration of how additional attentional demands can produced lateralised omissions (e.g. failing to take left-sided turns).

OVERVIEW

The apparent association between unilateral neglect and non-lateralised attentional difficulties outlined in the studies reviewed can now be set in the context of studies of hemispheric lateralisation of attentional function. In this chapter we have dealt with two important clinical diagnostic issues that, although conceptually separate from what is usually considered conventional neglect behaviours, are in practice closely linked to the clinical presentation of neglect. Sensory deficits may exaggerate or modify neglect; primary sensory and motor deficits may be mistaken for neglect. Since neglect is often associated with large right hemisphere lesions, and because the right hemisphere has a privileged role in certain types of attention, it is important to remember that neglect is often associated with more general and non-lateralised problems of attention. In Chapter 6 we will show how this close connection can result in useful therapeutic strategies which concentrate on modifying related attentional processes rather than directly targeting lateralised neglect.

CHAPTER THREE

Assessment of visual neglect

INTRODUCTION

Although there have been hundreds of neglect studies over the last 20 years, few employed standardised tests, and there is still much confusion among clinicians and researchers as to how the condition should be defined and assessed. This is particularly true given that many symptoms linked to neglect, such as extinction, allesthesia, and visual field deficits are only found on formal testing. Florid symptoms of neglect, however, can be easily observed in the ward, clinic or home without formal testing. Such patients as we saw in Chapter 1 may collide with objects on the left side, fail to eat from the left side of the plate, and only dress one side of the body. Objects and people may be completely ignored except when they are explicitly pointed out to the patient. Formal assessment of neglect is important, however, if therapists are to.

(a) quantify the extent and type of neglect;
(b) monitor changes in the condition;
(c) ensure that staff are discussing the same condition;
(d) evaluate the effects of rehabilitation or treatment.

TRADITIONAL TESTS OF VISUAL NEGLECT

Until recently, investigators of visual neglect have been hampered by a variety of unstandardised, often cross-modal, test procedures, all of which claim to measure the same underlying deficit. Given the multimodal range of clinical neglect phenomena and the absence of a single unifying theory, it is hardly surprising that there is no one "pure" test of neglect.

Testing has to be performed in various modalities to determine whether selective deficits are occurring within and across different sensory modalities. The two main features that characterise the clinical diagnosis of neglect are: (a) the failure to respond to particular events or objects (e.g. food on the left side of the plate, or the left sleeve of a jacket); (b) the spatial loci where the failure occurs: this part of space is commonly defined as "contralesional" (opposite the side of the lesion)—and usually refers to the body or space around the body.

As we saw in Chapter 1, neglect is best described as an "umbrella term" covering many different types of spatial attentional problems linked to omissions or failures in several different spatial domains.

Most of the cases described in Chapter 1 showed problems with "peripersonal" neglect; that is, patients tended to neglect objects and people located on the left side of reaching space. Traditionally, the assessment of unilateral neglect has largely been confined to paper and pencil tests in peripersonal space. Although there are now some 60 different tests of visual neglect, most are variants of the traditional and clinically well established bedside tasks such as line bisection, cancellation, copying, and drawing.

For clinical purposes, laterally impaired performance on any one measure (and in particular line bisection and cancellation) is usually regarded as supporting the diagnosis of neglect. Despite content and procedural differences all tests claim to be measuring (in some shape or form) aspects of the same disorder. As visual neglect may be present on some but not all tests at the same time (Weinstein & Friedland, 1977b), however, in practice it is best to use more than one type of test.

As we saw in Chapter 2, neglect and related problems are more common after right rather than left brain damage. Lack of agreement regarding the type of assessment to be used has made it difficult to establish a reliable incidence of neglect and compare the results of different studies. The proportion of right brain damaged patients suffering from neglect has accordingly varied greatly (cf Fig. 1.9, p. 13) and depends on the tests used, the time post onset, and aetiology involved.

The wide range of incidence figures also reflects the use of several different tests and different groups of patients. Most of these tests rely on paper and pencil desktop tests capable of assessing visual and motor aspects of peripersonal neglect. Patients are typically considered to have neglect if they miss more on one side of their body (usually the left in right brain damaged patients). Until a few years ago, therapists and clinicians relied on several unstandardised tests ranging from simple bedside copying tasks (Fig. 3.1) to sophisticated research tools involving divided visual field and computerised presentations (Fig. 3.2).

FIG. 3.1 The simple copying test used for the informal assessment of visual neglect.

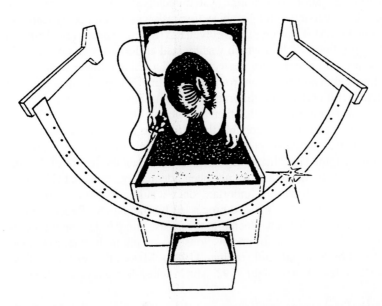

FIG. 3.2 Computerised testing for neglect. Reproduced with permission of W.B. Saunders Company from Anton, H.A., Hershler, H.C., Lloyd, P., and Murray, D. (1988). Visual neglect and extinction: A new test. *Archives of Physical Medicine and Rehabilitation*, *69*, 1014.

Line bisection as a measure of neglect

Of all the clinical tests used to diagnose visual neglect, requiring the patient to bisect or divide a horizontal line in half is by far the most simple and one of the oldest clinical test used (Halligan, 1995). In line bisection, the patient is required to estimate and then mark (in free vision) the mid-point of a line (using their non-affected hand). The page on which the line is presented is usually placed directly in front of the patient's mid-saggital plane and one line per page should ideally be presented. This ensures that the two main coordinate frames of reference, the trunk and head, are suitably aligned and that the effects of performance on previously bisected lines on the page do not interfere with subsequent performance.

The advantage of line bisection lies in its simplicity and its ease of quantification and repeatability. Although the results of line bisection initially suggest a comparatively straightforward and measurable indication of the patients' deviation to the right of true centre, several studies have shown that this simple explanation is far from the whole story.

The effect of line length.   Several studies (e.g. Halligan and Marshall, 1988) have reported that in most right brain damaged patients the extent of deviation is proportional to the line length. In other words, the longer the line the greater the deviation. To examine systematically the effect of line length a new quantifiable version of the line bisection task was developed by Halligan and Marshall (1988). This comprised eleven (25–279mm) or ten (18–180mm) different length lines, each of which was located at the centre of an A4 page. Using this test, all patients with neglect showed a reliable linear relationship between line length and deviation from centre of line. The performance of five such patients with unilateral right brain damage is shown in Fig. 3.3.

It can be seen from Fig. 3.3 that there is a gradual increase in deviation the longer the line. It can also be seen that the rate of increase varies considerably from patient to patient; however, in all cases, the extent of deviation is proportional to line length. This "linear relationship" between the length of the line and the extent of the deviation has not been adequately explained (Halligan, 1995). However, the finding is important since it suggests that in some sense the extent of the *whole line* may be processed by the patient. Recent studies have suggested that what is neglected in these cases may in fact be implicitly processed. Further evidence for unconscious processing in the case of neglect was described by Marshall and Halligan (1988). Many other examples have been reported (Berti & Rizzolatti 1992; McGlinchey-Berroth et al.,1994).

Bisection of short lines.   If there is a relationship between line length and extent of deviation such that bigger lines tend to show greater deviations, what happens with short lines? Does the patient get better or does he/she show

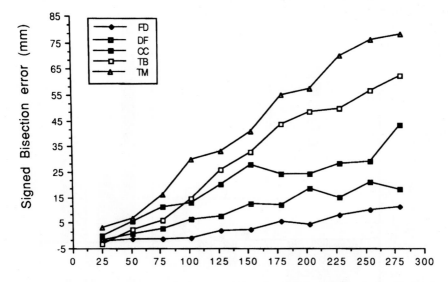

FIG. 3.3   The relationship between line length and bisection deviation in five patients with visual neglect. Reproduced with permission of The British Psychological Society from Halligan, P.W. (1995). Drawing attention to neglect: The contribution of line bisection. *The Psychologist, 8,* 257–264.

normal performance? It can be seen from Fig. 3.4 that patients were more accurate on short lines. It is difficult to see from this figure, however, that some patients in fact "cross over", that is show *right neglect* (left-sided deviation beyond normal control performance) when bisecting very short line lengths. (e.g. Halligan and Marshall, 1988). The performance of 6 patients with neglect and 18 normal controls on 3 lines of length 25, 51 and 77mm respectively, are shown in Fig. 3.4.

The finding that bisection performance in many patients is more accurate and even directionally different on short lines confirms the standard clinical practice of employing relatively large lines when assessing neglect. Although no previous published evidence suggests that bisection performance would cross over with shorter lines, it is likely that the conventional clinical use of long lines arose in part from the clinical experience that shorter lines were less sensitive indicators.

The effect of spatial location.   Most clinical studies of line bisection position the page and line directly in front of the patient's midline. If visual neglect occurs with respect to this reference frame—centred on body midline (with trunk and head relatively constrained)—then one might expect neglect to be comparatively more severe when lines are located in left hemispace and less

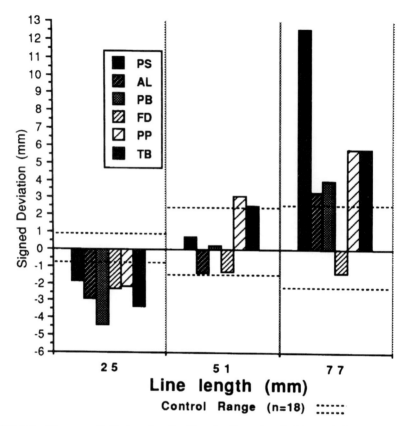

FIG. 3.4   "Cross over" effect on short line bisection. Reproduced with permission of The British Psychological Society from Halligan, P.W. (1995). Drawing attention to neglect: The contribution of line bisection. *The Psychologist, 8,* 257–264.

severe when they were located in right hemispace, a finding reported by many researchers.

The effects of three spatial locations (left, middle, and right) for the same line lengths (203mm) positioned on a standard A4 page can be readily seen in Fig. 3.5. This data, collected from 93 unilateral brain damaged patients and 40 age-matched controls seen at Rivermead Rehabilitation Center using their right hand, used the three lines from the Behavioural Inattention Test (BIT) (Wilson, 1987).

The 93 stroke patients had all sustained unilateral strokes within 6 months of testing. Twenty-five patients had strokes affecting the left hemisphere; the remaining 68 had right hemisphere strokes. The severity of their visual neglect was independently derived from their performance on the five other tests of the

BIT: line, letter, and star cancellation, figure and shape copying and drawing from memory. On the basis of their aggregate scores and comparisons with age-matched controls, patients were assigned to the following groups: (a) no discernible neglect [N-], (b) mild lateralised neglect [N+], and (c) moderate to severe lateralised neglect [N++] (See Fig. 3.5)

The data in Fig. 3.5 are remarkably regular. Overall presentation centred in left space shifts the majority of transactions rightwards while presentation in right space shifts performance leftwards. Midline presentation shows a small left bias in controls, an effect that is marginally increased in left brain damaged patients with visual neglect. Right brain damaged patients without neglect show a small rightward bias, an effect that increases threefold in patients with mild neglect and tenfold in patients with moderate to severe neglect.

Until recently, little data was available on the effect of similar hemispatial position for reading tasks. A single case reported by Cubelli, Pugliese, and Gabellini (1994) found that while line bisection performance was significantly more accurate in right space as compared with left and centre, the opposite result was found when a similar task involving reading was employed. In other words, reading was significantly more accurate when the words to be read were presented on the left side than in the centre or right side.

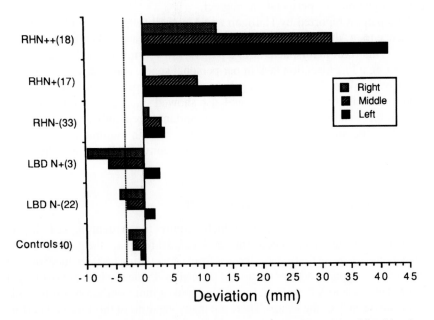

FIG. 3.5   The effects of spatial position on the page in a large group study of line bisection. Reproduced with permission of The British Psychological Society from Halligan, P.W. (1995). Drawing attention to neglect: The contribution of line bisection. *The Psychologist, 8,* 257–264.

The effect of different spatial domains.   Most clinical studies of line bisection involve the presentation of stimuli within reaching space. For the most part, neglect refers to the patient's response within peripersonal space on the affected side. As mentioned in Chapter 1, neglect can affect personal (or "body") space, peripersonal space (stimuli within reaching and grasping distance), and extrapersonal space (stimuli beyond arm's reach). Patients with personal neglect may fail to recognise their own paretic limb or may *under-use* the limb in question. It is in peripersonal space, (within arm's reach) where most neglect phenomena is observed and studied. Extrapersonal space refers to areas beyond arm's reach where the patient's responses is limited to pointing, naming, or throwing. Many patients show neglect in both personal and peripersonal spatial domains; some, however, show neglect in one but not the other.

Bisiach, Perani, Vallar, and Berti (1986) reported one such "dissociation" between personal neglect (patients were required to touch the affected left hand with the right hand) and peripersonal neglect (patients were required to cancel targets on a page in front of them). In 1992, Guariglia and Antonucci reported the opposite "dissociation" in the case of a patient who had severe personal neglect in the absence of peripersonal neglect. This suggests the existence of independent map systems for exploring distinct parts of space. Until recently it was not certain whether far extrapersonal space was compromised or spared in cases of personal or peripersonal neglect.

The patient reported by Halligan and Marshall (1991b) provided the first evidence for a "dissociation" between peripersonal space and far extrapersonal space. This right hemisphere stroke patient showed marked left-sided visual neglect on a line bisection task in peripersonal space, and is described in Box 1.7, Chapter 1 (p. 30). A second patient with severe peripersonal neglect was also tested with the same method and also showed significant improvement in far extrapersonal space. Therefore, it is important to remember that severe left visual neglect in peripersonal space can co-exist with minimal neglect in far extrapersonal space (see Fig. 3.6). Recently, the converse dissociation has been reported by Vuilleumier et al. (1998).

Cancellation as a measure of neglect

Cancellation tests are measures which require the patient to search and (usually) indicate (mark) specific targets located throughout the page. The type of response measure that can be derived from cancellation tasks include: degree of accuracy, speed, and the location of the errors. Typically in the case of right brain damage and left neglect, the patient makes more omissions on the side opposite the side of the lesion. There are many versions of this test, and performance has been shown to vary depending on the stimulus content, whether the task is timed, the number of distracting stimuli, the spatial locations of the targets, the density of stimuli, and the distance between stimuli (Kaplan et al.,

Near/Far

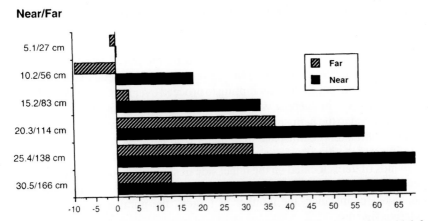

FIG. 3.6   The differential effects of near and far space on line bisection in a patient with left neglect.

1991). Performance can also be scored in terms of the amount of time taken to complete the task; however, in severe cases a fast performance may be indicative of severe neglect—this occurs because the patient ignores the left stimuli!

Clinical experience suggests that the pressure to perform the task within a designated time usually produces more omissions and, therefore, can be useful in those patients who appeared to have recovered. In scoring performance on these tasks, it is possible to obtain a qualitative picture of the patient's performance by charting the approximate response pattern used.

Gauthier, Dehaut, and Joanette (1989) describes such a method of charting patient's performance using their "Bell Cancellation Test". In this case, the examiner who is positioned opposite the patient, traces the sequence of cancellations by numbering the bells in chronological order. Patients with neglect typically cancel the targets located on one side of the stimulus page. If neglect is a deficit in attention systems directed toward contralateral hemispace, then it is possible that the normal clinical practice (of right hand on the right side) increases the overall presentation of neglect on the left side.

If patients with left-sided neglect are strongly attracted to targets situated on the non-neglected right side, then permitting them to begin the task with their right hand on the right side of the page may maintain the patient's attention to those previously crossed out targets located on the right side. The study by Mark, Kooistra, and Heilman (1988) examined this hypothesis in ten patients with neglect using two versions of a cancellation test. The first version involved the standard clinical presentation; patients were required to cancel all the targets by crossing them out (i.e. drawing over them). The second version involved erasing the targets. These researchers found that there were significantly more omissions using the traditional crossing out version (the first version) than the second, erasing, version. The improvement when target lines were removed from the right during the second task suggests that the presentation of neglect on such tasks is influenced by the initial lateralised strategy (right-sided start) together with the co-presence of cancelled stimuli in non-neglected hemispace while attempting to proceed over into the neglected field.

This result is in keeping with Posner et al.'s (1984) findings, namely, that cues to attend to the hemispace ipsilateral to the lesion slow responses to targets in the contralateral hemispace in patients with parietal injury. Other findings confirm that the degree of neglect observed is a function of the overall attention demands of items located on the intact side of space. In addition, the nature and number of patterns used in these tasks may in turn influence the severity of neglect—for instance, the number of targets, the number of foils, and their relative spacing.

Copying as a measure of neglect

Stars, cubes, Greek crosses, clock faces, and flowers are some of the many objects of line drawing that have been used as stimuli for patients with neglect to copying. Not all patients with neglect, however, show problems on this type of test. Where they do, their performance can contain some of the most memorable and striking illustrations of how neglect can effect a patient's constructive visual motor processes. This includes omissions or distortions of all or some of the lateral features of the figures to be copied. Marshall and Halligan (1993) devised a simple copying test that is capable of demonstrating different types of visuospatial neglect. The stimuli consisted of one figure (a flowering plant) which could be transformed into two complex figures by *deleting* selective parts of the original drawing. The task performance of five patients with left neglect is shown in Fig. 3.7. These copies illustrate the varied spatial "reference frames" within which visual neglect may be manifest.

Drawing as a measure of neglect

Drawing and constructional tasks remain some of the clearest ways of illustrating the curious and often variable nature of visual neglect. Drawing, in particular, is often used to illustrate the most striking demonstrations of neglect. When drawing from memory, patients tend to confine their drawings to the right side of the page; the drawings themselves often include adequate representations of the right side of the object but with the left side either omitted entirely or grossly distorted. An additional characteristic of many patients with neglect is their apparent lack of awareness of the deficit (see discussion on the phenomenon of completion in Chapter 2). Even when the incongruity of their asymmetric productions or behaviours is repeatedly pointed out to them, patients may persist in their neglect, often minimising or rationalising the omission.

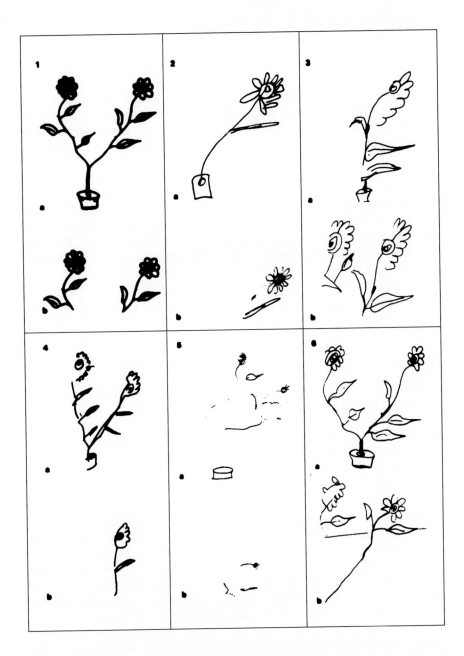

FIG. 3.7   Flower copying task. Reproduced with permission of Springer-Verlag from Marshall, J.C., and Halligan, P.W. (1993). Visuo-spatial neglect: A new copying test to assess perceptual parsing. *Journal of Neurology, 240,* 37–40.

Imaginal recall as a measure of neglect

As we saw in Chapter 1, some patients with visual neglect show neglect of internally generated images. Since the first reports by Bisiach and Luzzatti, back in 1978, several researchers have replicated this striking phenomenon. One group of German researchers used a task where patients were required to describe from memory those countries bordering the former West Germany. In another study, Italian patients were asked to imagine and describe three major squares in Rome with which they were all familiar. Meador, Loring, Bowers, and Heilman (1987) showed that physical orientation of the patient's head and eyes increased the numbers of items recalled in some patients. Probably the simplest tests to assess imaginal neglect is the "The O'Clock Test" by Grossi, Angelini, Pecchinenda, and Pizzamiglio (1993). Although this form of neglect is usually found in association with neglect on visuospatial tasks, not all patients with neglect on visuospatial tasks show imaginal neglect. Recently, cases have been reported (Guariglia et al., 1993; Beschin et al., 1997) who only showed neglect on imagery tasks. Unlike the patients described by Bisiach and Luzzatti (1978), who showed imaginary neglect for the Piazza del Duomo in Milan, these patients showed no evidence of neglect in personal or extra-personal space.

The Balloons Test: a new screening test of neglect

As seen in Chapter 2, some patients learn to compensate for their neglect by scanning to the left side, particularly on paper and pencil tests, despite continuing to show neglect in other activities of everyday life. A recent test, the Balloons Test (Edgeworth, Robertson, & MacMillan, 1998) is sensitive to unilateral neglect, particularly among patients who may be compensating for the deficit yet who still have underlying problems. This test can therefore be useful as a screening test leading on to a fuller assessment using the Behavioural Inattention Test.

This test uses the finding from cognitive psychology that certain types of stimuli need to be actively searched for among a cluster of other stimuli, whereas others "pop out" automatically. Neglect for the former tends to be much greater than for the latter. For instance, detecting a red circle among a lot of blue circles is easy as the red "pops out", whereas detecting the letter P among a lot of letters R is difficult and requires active search. In the Balloons Test, these two types of search are contrasted: in the easy "pop-out" search, a number of "balloons" (circles with lines coming out of the bottom) have to be found scattered among a series of other circles with no lines (Fig. 3.8, top). This is quite easy to do, and neglect patients miss less targets compared to the other condition, where some circles are scattered among a lot of balloons (Fig. 3.8, bottom).

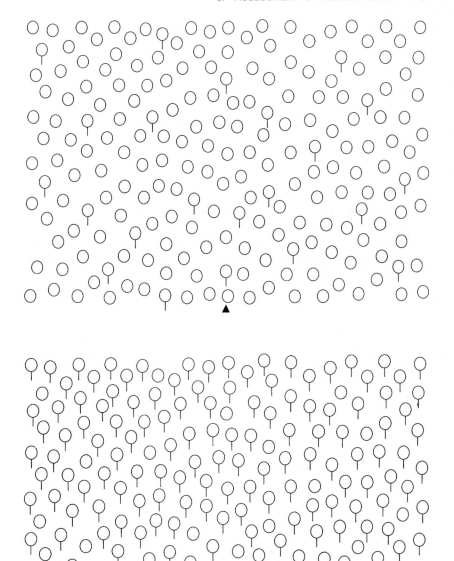

FIG. 3.8   The Balloons Test. Reproduced with permission of Thames Valley Test Company, Bury St. Edmunds, UK.

Another advantage of the Balloons Test is that it allows the exclusion of a visual field defect as the primarily cause of omissions on the left side. If more errors are made on the main task compared to the control task, then we can be sure that neglect figures in the problem, as the tests are visually very similar.

Need for standardised ecological measures of neglect

A major limitation of computerised and many conventional clinical tests is that when used on their own, they fail to capture the wide range of lateralised perfor- mance that characterises the condition and neglect clinically. Another limita- tion concerns the need to relate performance on these tests to the patient's functioning in their everyday environment.

Since the consequences of neglect can vary from patient to patient, routine clinical assessments often fail to detect the specific problems the patient has in his or her own environment. For the planning of rehabilitation, therefore, it is important to carry out observations of the patient's behaviour in real life situa- tions, in addition to using standardised assessments. For instance, in John's case (Case 1 in Chapter 1, pp. 4–6), as well as showing neglect on formal tests, he also bumped into objects and missed food on the left side of his plate. In order to provide clinicians with a more behaviourally relevant measure of visual neglect in peripersonal space, Wilson, Cockburn, and Halligan (1987) devised and standardised the Behavioural Inattention Test (BIT) (Wilson, 1987). Behavioural measures provide a useful instrument for evaluating a patient's functional performance irrespective of the theoretical orientation adopted. This test battery which was specifically designed to evaluate visual spatial neglect in peripersonal space and includes two qualitatively different sets of tests; six "conventional" tests and nine "behavioural" tests. The conven- tional tests include many measures of neglect that have been traditionally used in neurology and neuropsychology to assess neglect.

THE BEHAVIOURAL INATTENTION TEST (BIT)

This battery, which was standardised using 80 stroke patients and 50 age-matched controls, consists of six "conventional" tests of neglect and nine "behavioural" tests of neglect based on more realistic situations such as reading menus and searching for coins. The six conventional tests are: line cancellation, letter cancellation, star cancellation, figure and object copy, line bisection, and representational drawing. Three of the conventional subtests are described and illustrated in Figs 3.9, 3.10, and 3.11.

Line crossing.   This visual search test requires the patient to detect and cross out all the target lines on the page. The examiner demonstrates the required response by crossing out two of the four lines located in the central column, and then instructs the subject to cross out all the lines he or she can see on the page (Fig. 3.9). The four central lines are not scored. Contralateral, ipsilateral, or more diverse patterns of omission can be detected using the score sheet provided.

Star cancellation.   The star cancellation test consists of a page containing a random array of verbal and non-verbal stimuli. The patient is instructed to cancel all the "small" stars from this array of distractors (Fig. 3.10). Two examples of the small stars are pointed out to the patient. The task is to locate and cross out all the 54 small stars (6mm × 6mm) randomly interspersed with 52 large stars, 13 randomly positioned letters, and 10 short words. The maximum scores is 54: 27 left, 27 right.

Figure and shape copying.   This is one of the simplest and most common of clinical tests used to elicit visual neglect. The patient is instructed to copy three separate, simple drawings from the left side of the page (Fig. 3.11). In those cases where the patient has to use their non-preferred hand, a copy of the stimulus sheet is positioned directly above the response sheet, to ensure that

FIG. 3.9   Line crossing task from the BIT. Reproduced with permission of Thames Valley Test Company, Bury St. Edmunds, UK.

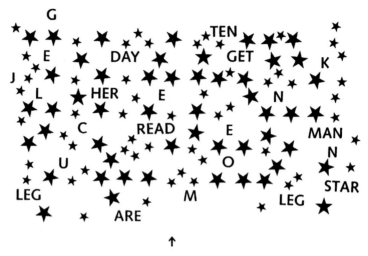

FIG. 3.10   Star cancellation from the BIT. Reproduced with permission of Thames Valley Test Company, Bury St. Edmunds, UK.

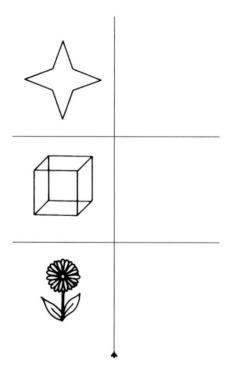

FIG. 3.11   Figure and shape copying from the BIT. Reproduced with permission of Thames Valley Test Company, Bury St. Edmunds, UK.

the patient's left hand does not obscure the target stimulus when copying. The three drawings, a four-pointed star, a cube, and a daisy, are arranged vertically and are clearly indicated to the patient. The second part of the test requires the patient to copy a group of three geometric shapes presented on a separate stimulus sheet. Unlike the previous items, the contents of this page are not pointed out to the patient.

Scoring the conventional BIT subtests

The six subtests of the BIT have all been shown to intercorrelate highly. However, subsequent research has indicated that while it is clinically meaningful to cluster the impairments as a common deficit, the underlying mechanism impaired may be far from unitary (Halligan, Marshall, & Wade, 1989).

Scores from the BIT subtests can be used to calculate an aggregate score for the six tests. Points are given for correct performance, thus higher scores indicate better performance. A score at or below 129 on the 6 conventional tests (i.e. below the worst controls) is used to indicate that a patient has an attentional problem which requires further investigation on the behavioural tests.

An alternative way of scoring, which has the advantage of providing specific information about the potential different types of neglect involved, is to note the number of tests (using the individual test cut-off) on which inattention is present, as shown in Table 3.1 A patient scoring above 129 but falling at or below the cut-off score for one or more of the *individual* conventional subtests should also be assessed with the behavioural subtests. Results from the latter would then provide a clearer picture of the way a particular patient's neglect manifests itself in everyday life.

Laterality of omissions on the BIT

It is clinically recognised that different patterns of omission can result from unilateral brain damage. These omissions may involve targets other than those located on the contralateral side of space. Chen Sea, Henderson, and Cermak

TABLE 3.1
Cut-off scores for conventional subtests of BIT

Subtest	Acceptable range	Cut-off scores
Line crossing	35–36	34
Letter cancellation	33–40	32
Star cancellation	52–54	51
Figure and shape copy	4	3
Line bisection	8–9	7
Representational drawing	3	2
Total		129

(1993) have shown that the distinction between lateralised and non-lateralised forms of inattention may have important functional implications. In their study the relationship between patterns of visual spatial inattention and activities of daily living (ADL) performance was investigated in 64 patients with right brain lesions, using an ADL scale and a Chinese Word Cancellation Test. Patients demonstrating lateralised inattention were significantly worse on measures of ADL performance compared with patients with non-lateralised inattention. Independence in dressing, mobility, and toileting were more adversely affected by hemi-inattention than bathing/hygiene, eating, and telephone use.

Although the BIT was primarily devised to facilitate the evaluation of hemi-inattention or unilateral neglect, the test is concerned with the measurement of spatial inattention wherever it occurs on the stimulus page. Although not explicitly indicated in the manual, the extent of lateralised and non-lateralised neglect shown on each of the BIT tests can be calculated relatively easily, and is described later in this chapter.

Interpreting the conventional subtests

When assessing neglect, it is important to consider other associated cognitive deficits, together with general mental and sensory motor functioning. As with all assessments, it is important to observe the manner in which the patient performs the task. For example, patients with visual neglect typically begin from the right or sometimes the middle part of the page. Within the attended side of space they also tend to position their drawings or copies very close to the edge of the page. Errors of commission are also occasionally encountered.

Behavioural tests of the BIT

The behavioural tests of the BIT include the following: picture scanning, telephone dialling, menu reading, article reading, telling and setting the time, coin sorting, address and sentence copying, map navigation and card sorting. Three of the nine behavioural tests of the BIT are discussed below.

Picture scanning.   In this test, three large photographs, each measuring 357 x 278mm are presented one at a time and depict: (1) a meal; (2) a wash basin and toiletries; (3) a large room flanked by various pieces of furniture and hospital aids (Fig. 3.12). The patient is instructed to name and/or point to the main items in the picture. Each photograph is placed in front of the seated patient who is not permitted to move it. Omissions are scored, although errors of identification are noted. The scoring of this and all subsequent tests is out of a total of nine. Points are subtracted from this maximum score for errors and is calculated from the total number of omissions recorded.

FIG. 3.12   Picture scanning task from the BIT. Reproduced with permission of Thames Valley Test Company, Bury St. Edmunds, UK.

Menu reading.   This task consists of an 'open-out' page (420 x 297mm) containing 18 common food items arranged in 4 adjacent columns (2 on the left and 2 on the right) (Fig. 3.13). The food items are presented in 6mm high letters. Each of the 18 items is scored as correct or incorrect. Incorrect responses refer to partial/whole word substitutions or omission.

Telling and setting the time.   This test has three parts. The first requires the subject to read the time from photographed settings on a digital clock face. Secondly, the patient is required to read the time from three settings on an analogue clock face. Finally, the patient is requested to set times on the analogue clock face as they are called out by the examiner (Fig. 3.14).

Scoring of the behavioural subtests

As with the conventional subtests, both the overall behavioural score and the individual subtests scores can be considered. A total score at or below 67, or scores at or below the cut-off on one or more individual subtests can suggest attentional difficulties due to neglect (Table 3.2).

Among the BIT subtests, it is not uncommon to find differences both within and between patients. Some patients show impairments on the representational

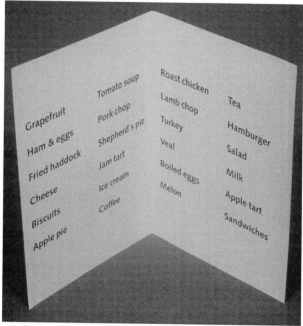

FIG. 3.13   Menu reading task from the BIT. Reproduced with permission of Thames Valley Test Company, Bury St. Edmunds, UK.

FIG. 3.14   Time reading task from the BIT. Reproduced with permission of Thames Valley Test Company, Bury St. Edmunds, UK.

TABLE 3.2
Cut-off scores for behavioural subtests (BIT)

Subtest	Acceptable range	Cut-off scores
Picture scanning	6–9	5
Telephone dialling	8–9	7
Menu reading	9	8
Article reading	9	8
Tell/set time	9	8
Coin sorting	9	8
Address and sentence	8–9	7
Map navigation	9	8
Card sorting	9	8
Total		129

drawing, for instance, yet demonstrate little difficulty on the cancellation tasks. The converse is also true, and in general, variation in performance on this range of subtests can often conceal a wide range of different underlying types of neglect. For the time being, however, the BIT remains one of the most comprehensive test batteries currently available.

The BIT is able to predict which stroke patients are likely to have everyday problems arising from visual neglect and has been shown to be both reliable and valid. In addition to the checklist used in the original validation, additional studies to determine whether the BIT actually relates to functional performance, have been reported by Sheil (1990) and by Hartman-Maeir and Katz (1994). The results of Hartman-Maeir and Katz are summarised in Fig. 3.15.

Sheil (1990) showed that there was a strong association between neglect performance on the BIT and Activities of Daily Living (ADL) as measured by the Rivermead ADL Assessment and Frenchay Activities Index. The study by Hartman-Maeir and Katz (1994) set out to establish the predictive validity of the behavioural subtests and to check whether patients classified as showing neglect on the conventional tasks could be distinguish by the behavioural tests. The finding that most (7/9) of the tests could discriminate significantly between those patients with and without neglect supports the validity of the behavioural subtests.

Furthermore, they found a significant relationship between performance on the behavioural tests and performances on actual tasks and an ADL checklist. The BIT norms allow therapists to focus on those areas of everyday life which have given rise to particular problems for the patient. Hopefully, in the future it will be possible to explain the dissociations, which often appear among the different subtests in the current battery.

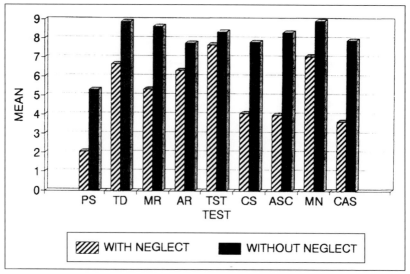

BIT Behavioural Subtests: Comparison between group with neglect and group without neglect. PS = Picture Scanning, TD = Telephone Dialling, MR = Menu Reading, AR = Article Reading, TST = Telling and Setting Time, CS = Coin Sorting, ASC = Address and Sentence Copying, MN = Map Navigation, CAS = Card Sorting.

FIG 3.15   Comparison of patients with and without neglect on the Behavioural subtests of the BIT. From Hartman-Maeir, A., and Katz, N. (1995). Validity of the Behavioral Inattention Test (BIT): Relationships with functional tasks. *American Journal of Occupational Therapy, 49,* 507–516. Copyright 1995 by the American Occupational Therapy Association, Inc. Reprinted with permission.

CLINICAL OBSERVATIONS
OF TEST PERFORMANCE

A number of clinical aspects need to be borne in mind, however, when analysing and interpreting the results of the BIT and other tests of neglect.

Dissociations between different tests.   Dissociations in performance occur whereby on one test a patient performs within normal limits yet on another test clearly shows neglect. John, the first case described in Chapter 1 (pp. 4–6), made 30 omissions on star cancellation, but on the line bisection he showed normal performance. When drawing a butterfly from memory, Veronica (Case 4 in Chapter 1, pp. 8–10) copied the figures adequately, but on reading from the BIT, she missed most of the words on the left side of the page. Dissociations of this sort are not uncommon. There are many different reasons why people perform badly on one test, but not on another. One possible reason concerns individual patient fluctuations in arousal and attention, another is the type of neglect, and a third concerns the particular demands of the task. Hence, clinicians should not be surprised to find variations in patient performance from test to test.

Extent of laterality.   Traditionally, studies of spatial neglect after right hemisphere brain damage have assumed that most of the omissions will be on the left side. A more detailed examination of John's performance on star cancellation showed that in addition to left side omissions, he also tended to make omissions on the right side of the star cancellation task. It is not unusual to find patients who, while showing left neglect on many tasks, show right neglect on some others, as described in Chapter 2. Right brain damaged patients showing right (ipsilesional) errors have often been ignored or removed from previous analysis. Findings (Sirigu, Grafman, Bressler, & Sunderland, 1991) suggest the need to quantify and document the number and location of all omissions, wherever they occur. Previous studies of neglect have used different criteria to indicate the number and spatial locations of omissions. Most traditional tests of neglect use the patient's mid-saggital plane, which is usually aligned with the objective centre of the stimulus page, as the criterion from which to define left/right omissions.

However, some researchers have not specified how lateralisation on these tasks should be quantified. For example, Albert (1973), who published one of the first standardised tests of visual neglect, defined neglect on his line-crossing task as the presence of any omission irrespective of location. In an attempt to quantify the asymmetrical performance in neglect, some researchers have developed indices (Friedman, 1992) for the degree of lateralisation. These indices can provide useful information as to the lateralised extent and severity of the omissions involved.

In the case of the six conventional tests of the BIT, it is possible to employ a simple lateralised scoring system. Total performance on each of the six subtests provides the initial diagnosis of what can be termed "attentional impairment". This is derived from the age-matched controls provided (Halligan, Cockburn & Wilson, 1991). Patients initially diagnosed as showing attentional impairment, irrespective of the position of the errors, can then be analysed for the degree of spatial lateralisation. Figure 3.16 shows the range of scores of stroke patients on the star cancellation task subtest. The X axis represents the laterality index range, the larger vertical hashed line represents the non-lateralised performance, and the horizontal hashed line represents normal performance.

To obtain a measure of the distribution of omissions/errors on the six tests, a simple laterality index can be calculated. In the case of right brain damaged patients, this involves dividing the total number of targets correctly cancelled or drawn on the left side of the page by the total number of targets cancelled or drawn on the whole test (line crossing, letter cancellation, star cancellation, and the two drawing tasks). Using this method, it is possible to calculate values ranging from 0.0 (severe contralesional neglect) to 1.0 (severe ipsilesional neglect), with values close to 0.5 suggesting bilateral or symmetrical

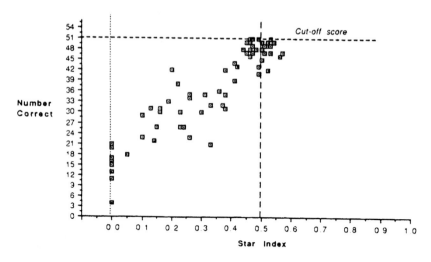

FIG. 3.16 Laterality distribution on star cancellation (see text for details). Reprinted with permission of Psychology Press Limited, Hove, UK from Halligan, P.W., et al. (1991b). The laterality of visual neglect after right hemisphere damage. *Neuropsychological Rehabilitation, 1,* 281–301.

performance. In other words, the more score values differ from 0.5 the more a patient shows bias towards the right or left. In the case of line bisection, the index consists of both the extent and direction of deviation for all three lines. The sum of the deviations in millimetres is calculated from true centre to the right, minus the sum of deviations in millimetres from true centre to the left. Although the pattern of performance suggests a continuum, it is possible to identify at least four basic patterns of spatial error from the laterality scores. The four basic patterns are as follows.

(a) *Contralateral neglect.* The patient omits relevant scorable features on the left side. The score index for such a patient is 0.0.
(b) *Left-sided inattention.* For this classification most of the patient's omissions are located on the contralesional side. The score index ranges between 0.1 and 0.47.
(c) *Non-lateralised inattention.* The patient in this case, must have omitted approximately equal numbers from both sides of the stimulus sheet. Accordingly, the score index ranges between 0.48 and 0.52.
(d) *Right-sided inattention.* For this classification, the patient omits more features on the right side of the stimulus. The score index for such patients is greater than or equal to 0.53.

The laterality extent for the line bisection task (using results from 50 normals) was as follows: left-sided inattention = right deviation greater than or equal to 39mm; non-lateralised inattention = left or right less than 39mm; right-sided inattention = deviation to the left greater than 39mm.

Neglect of far space.   As we showed in Chapter 1, cases have been identified where neglect of near space is significant, but neglect of objects or people in far space is not apparent. In practical terms, there are no currently standardised measures of neglect for far space. Stone et al. (1991b), however, describe a simple bedside technique that can be used to assess the patient's ability to detect objects in far space (see Fig. 3.17). In their test, they asked patients to point or name all the objects they could see on both sides of the hospital room or ward. The examiner stood directly behind the patient and made sure in advance that the distribution of objects on the left-hand and right-hand sides was roughly the same. Using a photocopy of a closed semicircle with the patients head marked in the centre of the base, the examiner noted which objects were situated at 0, 45, 90, 135, and 180° landmarks. As the patient pointed or named objects in the room, the examiner marked their approximate location and number of degrees.

It seems likely that a large proportion of patients with right hemisphere lesions may show neglect in both near and far space in the visual modality. However, there are some patients who clearly show differences in their neglect for near and far space, as we indicated in Chapter 1. One way this was demonstrated to us in the case of John (Case 1, pp. 4–6) was when as part of a patient outing, he took part in an air gun shooting range contest at a local fair. Despite

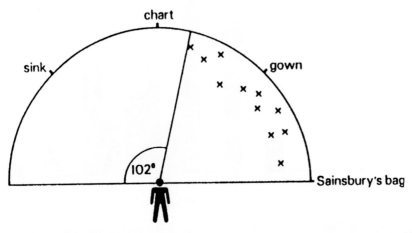

FIG. 3.17   A simple test of neglect of extrapersonal space (see text for details). Reprinted with permission of The Lancet Ltd from Stone, S.P., and Greenwood, R.J. (1991). *The Lancet, 337,* 114. © by The Lancet Ltd, 1991.

the fact that he showed significant omissions on most of the BIT subtests, John's performance targeting the bullseye which was located 15 feet away, revealed surprisingly accurate performance.

Input versus output neglect.   All the BIT tests require some motor response by patients. Consequently, the problem for a patient in a test such as star cancellation may not lie in moving their hands into the left half of space, but rather being aware of targets on the left side. There are few existing methods for assessing whether a person has primarily a problem in *attending* to stimuli on the left, or of *responding* to them. In Chapter 1 (Box 1.4, p. 22) we described Tegner's study, where this distinction was made using an experimental procedure. In an effort to distinguish between these two possible factors using a more clinically easier test, Milner devised the simple "landmark test". (Milner, Brechmann, Pagliarini 1992). This simple test can help distinguish between input (i.e. perceptual) and output (i.e. motor) neglect. An example of a patient showing such a dissociation is described in Fig. 3.18. (Marshall and Halligan, 1995b). The patient has to *judge* how central a line is versus actually moving the point to the centre of the line. The patient is more accurate with perceptual judgements than motor bisection; the latter are significantly to the right. In other words the "output" is more affected than the "input".

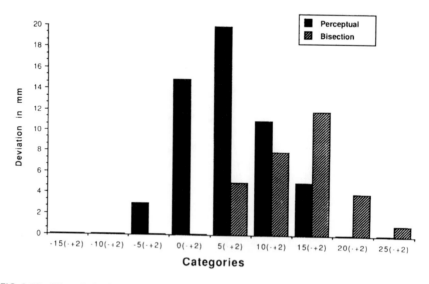

FIG. 3.18   Dissociation between perceptual and perceptual motor judgements on a line bisection task (see text for details). Reproduced with permission of Clinical Neurologica from Halligan, P.W., and Marshall, J.C. (1995b). Within- and between-task dissociations in visuospatial neglect: A case study. *Cortex, 31*, 367–376.

In practice, however, it is likely that most patients with large right hemisphere lesions show elements of both input and output neglect. The importance of distinguishing those patients with primarily input or output deficits in neglect, concerns the possible different treatment strategies that might be offered. These will be described in the following chapters.

Modified version of BIT for acute patients

It is not always possible to give the whole BIT, because of time constraints or limits in patient compliance. This is particularly true for acute patients seen in hospital wards. For this reason, a modified version of the BIT (Stone et al., 1991a) was validated and standardised with patients after acute stroke, using data from age-matched controls. This modified version of the BIT consists of the following tests: (1) pointing to objects located around the patient's room, (2) pointing to items of food on a plate (picture of plate of food from BIT), (3) reading a menu (from BIT), (4) crossing out all the lines on a stimulus page, (5) crossing out all the small stars on the BIT star cancellation task, (6) selecting denominations of coin from an array on a card (from BIT), (7) reading a newspaper article (for right hemisphere stroke patients only, adapted from BIT), and (8) copying drawings of a daisy, cube, and star from the left side of the page to the right side (left hemisphere stroke patients only, from BIT).

To establish a normal range of performance for each of these tests, 47 controls (mean age 71.6) were assessed. This control sample is on average 20 years older than the original BIT and is useful when testing older stroke patients. In addition to these tests, the authors noted qualitative symptoms associated with neglect performance. The most important of these relates to "right hand start"; this observation describes the predisposition of most patients even when reading groups of words to begin on the right-hand side.

In the next chapter we consider other assessments of neglect, including personal neglect, anosognosia, extinction, and neglect dyslexia.

CHAPTER FOUR

Further assessments of neglect and related disorders

INTRODUCTION

The previous chapter focused mainly on the assessment of *visual* neglect. As we saw in Chapter 1, however, there are several different types of neglect and neglect-related phenomena and it is to these, as well as to some other methods of assessing visual neglect, that we turn in this chapter.

ASSESSMENT OF PERSONAL NEGLECT

Personal neglect describes those neglect behaviours that directly involve parts of the patient's body, typically the side opposite the lesion. Until very recently, no standardised methods existed for the assessment of personal neglect. One clinical method for assessing personal neglect involves the use of three everyday objects, namely a comb, a pair of spectacles, and a masked razor (if a man) or powder compact (if a woman) (Zoccolotti & Judica, 1991). The patient is asked to demonstrate the use of these objects, and then using a rating scale the assessor indicates the extent to which the patient shows personal neglect for the left side of the head. More recently, the comb and razor procedures have been made more sensitive and has been quantified in two recent studies (Beschin & Robertson, 1997; McIntosh, Brodie, Beschin, and Robertson (in press); Robertson, Hogg, & McMillan, 1998. Instead of making a judgement about the degree to which the person is neglecting the left side of the body when using the comb and razor (powder compact in the case of women), the number of movements made to each side of the midline is counted over a fixed period of 30 seconds for each implement.

This highly reliable procedure produces scores which are very sensitive to personal neglect and may detect right brain damaged patients who have no neglect on conventional peripersonal visual neglect testing. The criterion for personal neglect used was derived from age-matched control subjects. No control subject showed a bias greater than the cut-off score specified. Furthermore, this measure correlates extremely highly with measures of functional independence, more highly indeed than measures of visual neglect. Personal neglect can also be assessed informally by observing patients in their wheelchairs, in their attempts to dress themselves, and in their personal grooming. The rating scale described above may well miss some particular kinds of personal neglect, and it is necessary to supplement this assessment with careful observations of the patient's other daily life behaviour. The following questions should be considered:

(1) Does the person's arm or leg become regularly caught up with objects? In Rachel's case (see Chapter 1), this was certainly true. Although she had some sensation in her left arm and leg, she showed very clear extinction for sensation on both her arm and leg and tended not to notice them, even though she had slight movement in both. She was in constant danger of hurting herself, and this was directly caused by personal neglect of the left side of her body.

(2) Is the person's clothing, hair, shaving, or make-up clearly disorganised or absent on one side? Some patients with personal neglect show clear abnormalities when dressing or grooming their left side; e.g. poor shaving or make-up on the left side, or other atypical and asymmetrical patterns.

COMPUTERISED MEASURES OF VISUAL NEGLECT

Several forms of computerised assessment of neglect have been described. Anton et al. (1988) reported a computer-controlled test of visual neglect that could also be used to measure extinction. The computerised test was developed and evaluated by testing patients with right hemisphere stroke. This test consisted of a series of unilateral or bilateral lights on a semicircular array to which the subject was required to respond by pushing a button. An illustration of the test set-up is shown in Fig. 3.2 (p. 59). A computer controlled the sequence of stimuli lights and stored the patient's responses. Results of the computer test were then compared to conventional occupational therapy and clinical tests.

A similar instrument capable of distinguishing visual field deficits and extinction was reported by Beis, André, and Saguez (1994). This computerised test allowed the examiner to control a sequence of unilateral and bilateral lights, and store responses. The instrument consisted of an array of light-emitting diodes (LEDs) set in a horizontal semicircle. The set up contained 64 LEDs, placed at regular intervals. The radius of the semicircle array was 75cm. The patient sat in front of the semicircle array in a darkened environment and was required to fixate gaze on the central LED, as illustrated in Fig. 4.1.

Two scanning tasks were carried out: one which alternated from right to left from the periphery to the centre; the other which simultaneously moved right and left from the periphery to the centre. The authors claim that the computerised testing makes it possible to detect both hemianopia and extinction during the same examination. Despite their comparative ease of presentation and automatic recording of responses, computerised assessments have obvious limitations for the clinical setting. Box 4.1 outlines an approach to computerised assessment of line bisection.

ASSESSMENT OF ANOSOGNOSIA

It has been known for over a century that many brain damaged patients can be unaware of or even deny some of the very deficits that impair their performance in every day life. Babinski (1914) used the term "anosognosia" to describe patients who appeared to be unaware of their hemiplegia. Anosognosia is a

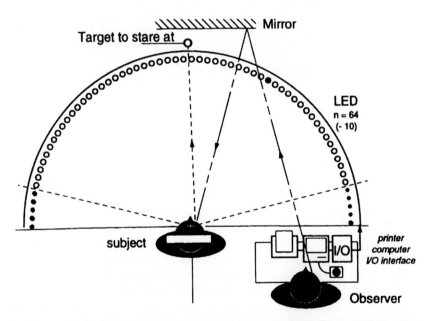

FIG. 4.1 Computerised procedure for assessing unilateral neglect and visual field deficits. Reproduced with permission of W.B. Saunders Company from Beis, J.-M., André, J.-M., & Saguez, A. (1994) Detection of visual field deficits and visual neglect with computerized light emitting diodes. *Archives of Physical Medicine and Rehabilitation*, 75, 711–713.

BOX 4.1   Computerised versions of line bisection

Several studies (Halligan & Marshall, 1989d, 1989c) investigated freehand line bisection performance with a computerised presentation in a patient with severe left neglect. In the computer format, the patient made transections with a "mouse"-controlled cursor arrow. The technique provided rigorous control over starting position and also allowed the patient to make self-corrections. Although left neglect persisted at longer line lengths under both conditions, the magnitude of the effect decreased significantly. Furthermore, the "cross-over point" where right displacements change to left displacements as a function of line length varied between the two conditions (freehand, computer-start).

Halligan and Marshall (1989d) also showed computerised line bisection could be used to distinguish between motor and perceptual aspects of line bisection. In the computerised format, the patient made her transections by moving a "mouse"-controlled cursor arrow. A display of the relevant conditions was shown in Chapter 1 (Fig. 1.13, p. 23).

In the perceptual condition, the direction of mouse movement and VDU cursor was the same. In order to distinguish possible pre-motor features, a second condition was employed which reversed the direction such that moving the mouse to the left caused the cursor arrow to move right and visa versa. Results from this reverse coupling suggested that hemispatial hypokinesia played little or no role in the interpretation of this patients results.

The technique also allows cueing (that is, the initial positioning of the cursor at either the left or right end of the stimulus line) to be locked to the task under analysis (line bisection). The effects of starting position and of perceptuo-motor compatibility upon the magnitude and direction of displacements from the true midpoint were compared and contrasted.

frequent complication of stroke found in over a third of stroke patients who can reliably respond to verbal questioning (Starkstein et al., 1993).

Anosognosia is commonly found in association with personal and peripersonal neglect. This lack of awareness can pose serious problems for rehabilitation, as such patients commonly fail to appreciate the relevance of remedial interventions and often overestimate their functional abilities.

Sometimes Victor (Case 3, pp. 7–8), when asked to move his left arm thought he was moving it. His fingers are able to make small twitching movements, but his arm remains still. When questioned about his affected arm he makes reference to what he feels to be a "third arm", although he is not clear about it. Box 4.2 describes an excerpt of Victor's account of these difficulties when questioned by one of the authors. Other examples of this type have been described (Halligan, Marshall, & Wade, 1993).

The underlying nature of anosognosia is still largely unknown. Unlike earlier psychodynamic models, recent "neurogenic" explanations have

BOX 4.2   Victor's lack of awareness

IR:	Tell me what problems you have had since your stroke?
Victor:	Principally physical ones. Not being able to walk, though I think this is partly psychological.
IR:	Could you explain?
Victor:	I can't walk primarily because of pain in my leg and hip. It's also a matter of confidence.
IR:	Can you move your left side?
Victor:	I have a partial paralysis.
IR:	Could you show me how much you can move your left hand?
Victor:	Normally.
IR:	Could you please lift it up for me?
Victor:	There you are [does not move the arm].
IR:	You're lifting it up?
Victor:	Yes, that's me lifting it up now [arm still located on left side].
IR:	Can you see your left hand lifted up?
Victor:	Yes.
IR:	Can you move your left hand and touch your right ear?
Victor:	OK [arm still located on left side].
IR:	Can you feel it touch your right ear?
Victor:	No, but I know it's there, judging by the approximate speed it went at and the time it took.
IR:	Do you have a feeling of your left arm being lifted up towards your right ear?
Victor:	Not really, it's more the time and the speed it took.
IR:	Are you doing it now?
Victor:	Yes.
IR:	Could you please look down and tell me what that is [IR touches Victor's paralysed left hand with his hand, and encourages him to look down at it].
Victor:	It's my left hand.
IR:	But I thought you were holding your left hand up at your ear?
Victor:	That's right, the problem is in distinguishing between *the* left hand and the next one.
IR:	So you've got two left hands?
Victor:	Yes, I have the impression of having two.
IR:	Just the hand, or the whole arm?
Victor:	The whole arm and hand.
IR:	Where is the other arm?
Victor:	I don't know.
IR:	So when you said you had moved your left arm, it was actually staying on your lap?
Victor:	That can often be the case.

attempted to characterise the disrupted cognitive functioning involved (Prigatano & Schacter, 1991; Levine, Calvanio, & Rinn, 1991). However, the study of anosognosia, like that of neglect, has been beset by important conceptual and methodological problems.

No clear-cut definition of anosognosia has been formulated, and the condition has only been recently measured or studied in conjunction with other aspects of neuropsychological or neurological function (Stone et al., 1992). Classifications of different types of anosognosia have been made using rating scales such as the one developed by Cutting (1978) or Starkstein et al. (1993).

Anosognosia can be selective; patients with more than one neurological problem due to brain damage may be anosognosic for some of them but not for others (Bisiach & Geminiani, 1991). Stroke patients with anosognosia may verbally admit (either spontaneously or in compliance with the examiner's diagnosis) to be hemiplegic yet ignore the consequences of such statements in planning and programming their subsequent functional motor activities (House & Hodges, 1988).

Anosognosia usually appears in the early stages after stroke and often fades away in the following weeks. While the acute manifestations of anosognosia are striking and appear to recover with time, it has been suggested that mild versions of the condition may exert important influences on the patient's behaviour several weeks, months, and even years post stroke.

Oddy, Coughlan, Typerman, and Jenkins (1985) studied patients' and families' descriptions of residual neuropsychological deficits seven years post brain damage and found that patients uniformly underestimated behavioural problems compared to the reports of their relatives. Relatives on the other hand, reported that the patients often seemed unrealistic and were usually unwilling to admit their residual deficits.

Although anosognosia may be present after right hemisphere stroke, there is no currently agreed set of measures that define this particularly striking form of behaviour. The patient's awareness of a deficit is central to any rehabilitative approach. People suffering from neglect do not behave as though they are experiencing partial perceptions; rather, they proceed as though they have an appropriate representation of themselves and their environment. The lack of awareness is important and, from a rehabilitation standpoint, is one of the major factors that can sustain disabilities long after physical deficits have recovered. Overcoming this lack of awareness lies at the heart of any successful rehabilitation program.

Despite several reports that denial or lack of awareness after brain damage can contribute to problems in rehabilitation planning, the area has received little attention from therapists and clinicians involved in patient treatment. In view of the theoretical and clinical implications of anosognosia, it would seem important for clinical management and neuropsychological research to develop an adequate description and understanding of the deficits involved.

Whether or not patients recover from neglect depends strongly on whether or not they are aware of their neglect. Victor (Case 3, pp. 7–8) suffers from anosognosia; he clearly is unable to appreciate some of the major consequences of his stroke. Clinicians should be aware that, like neglect, anosognosia does not appear to be an all or nothing phenomena; in other words, features of anosognosia can be selective. For instance, a patient may show it for hemianopia, but not hemiplegia. Furthermore, some patients may appear to accept, for instance, that their hands are paralysed, but at the same time state that they can tie their shoelaces or drive a car normally with both hands.

Like many other aspects of neglect assessment there is very little in the way of standardised assessment. One method, however, that has been used to assess anosognosia is described by Cutting (1978) and is shown in Box 4.3. This questionnaire shows the range of different types of phenomena that have been included under the condition. Furthermore, as can be seen from Box 4.4, far

---

BOX 4.3   Assessment of anosognosia (Adapted from Cutting, 1978)

General questions:
1. Do you know why you are in hospital?   yes/no
2. Do you know what has happened to you?   yes/no
3. Is there anything wrong with your arm or leg?   yes/no
4. Are they weak, paralysed, or numb?   yes/no
5. How does your arm/leg feel?

Further questions if denial elicited on general questions:
(examiner makes notes of answers)
1. *Picking up the affected arm*—What is that?
2. Can you lift it up for me?

3. Anosodiphoria	Is it a nuisance?
	Does it cause you much trouble?
	How do you feel about it?
Non-belonging	Do you ever feel that it does not belong to you?
	Do you feel it belongs to someone else?
Strange feelings	Do you feel the arm is strange or odd?
Misoplegia	Do you dislike/hate your arm?
Personification	Do you ever call it names?
Kinaesthetic hallucinations	Do you ever feel that it moves without your moving it yourself?
Supernumerary phantom limb	How many arms do you have?
	How many hands do you have?
	How many legs do you have?
	How many fingers do you have?
	Has any part of your body been added to or taken away as a result of your stroke?

BOX 4.4   A case of Somatoparaphrenia

Although some patients with right hemisphere stroke can show unawareness of their sensory and motor deficits (anosognosia), it is not uncommon for some patients to express abnormal beliefs about affected parts of the body. These patients show what have been described as "productive delusions" regarding the affected side. These productive delusions can include supernumerary phantom limb, reduplication of limbs, and somatoparaphrenia. A detailed description of a patient with somatoparaphrenia is described by Halligan, Marshall, and Wade (1995).

This 41-year-old man had suffered a stroke affecting his left-hand side. He mentioned to medical staff on several occasions that his left arm belonged to someone else, that he had a bag full of spare left arms, and that he was concerned that his left hand would die and disappear. These beliefs persisted for several months after his stroke. An excerpt of an interview with this patient is published below:

E: Can you raise your left arm?
P: *(Waves right arm)*. They took two fingers and joined them back together. The left hand, it's cut down the centre, but it still functions quite well. It's a nice hand.
E: What about your left leg?
P: It was very difficult to begin with......to live with a foot that isn't yours.
E: Why do you say that the foot is not yours?
P: I came to the conclusion that it was a cow's foot. And in fact I decided that they sewed it on. It looked and felt like a cow's foot, it was so heavy. But I adopted it. I'll take you home, I said.

from being unaware of the disorder, some patients may actually experience distortions and indeed additions to their body schema. In Box 4.4, an example of the type of delusion that may be present in these cases is reported in detail.

ASSESSMENT OF NEGLECT DYSLEXIA

As was seen with Veronica, (Case 4, pp. 8–10), neglect dyslexia is a disorder where reading problems are attributable to the patient's neglect. From an assessment point of view, there are two main types of neglect dyslexia—those involving the whole sentence or paragraphs, and those involving neglect of the left sides of single words. As was seen in Chapter 1, a patient may make meaningful substitutions for those parts of the words they are neglecting (e.g. for cream, dream), as well as omitting parts of them (e.g. smile, mile). The paragraph reading test from the BIT is sensitive to the former, and it is not unusual to find patients who miss out whole sections of the prose on the left side, or indeed those who miss out the whole left side column.

In 1987, Caplan devised a new reading test designed to be more sensitive at detecting left-sided neglect. The test consisted of an indented paragraph of 30 lines with a left-side margin intentionally constructed to be highly variable. An illustration of a similar type of test is shown in Fig. 4.2. The first word of each line was indented between 0 and 25 spaces, with the amount of indentation unpredictable from one line to the next. The right side was uniform. The

---

ASPECTS OF OXFORD

The ancient University City of Oxford, situated between the meandering Isis, Thames and the Cherwell Rivers has expanded north, south, east and west. It is a city of college spires, verdant parks and congested streets. Double-decker buses and low-loading coaches bully the cyclist on to the narrow pavements throughout the city. Pedestrians jostle each other as they wind their way to colleges, libraries, museums, galleries, offices, shops hospitals, eating houses, pubs and dentists. Hawkers selling ice-cream "Oxford University T-shirts" and sweaters, newspapers and paintings appear to have proprietary rights, cluttering the same pavements that tourist and locals find so scarce. The town and gown communities reside side by side. The students can be seen cycling or walking to and from examinations rooms, dressed in black and white with a shortened gown with strips for sleeves. The more flamboyant adopt a stance by flaunting a pink or red carnation as a buttonhole. The local hobos jeer and gesture with hands outstretched to all passersby asking for cash for food, but judging from the prevailing odour, this could be interpreted to mean drink. The homeless men and women, some refugees, sit by the stone walls of ancient buildings or doorways blocked and no longer in use, crude hand- written signs advertising their plight, hoping for some monetary aid. To escape from it all there is the entrance by a gateway into St John's College Quad where the peace and tranquility of a walled garden can be enjoyed. Notices remind all that students are at work in their rooms and quiet is required. Some seek out the chapel to sit on the wooden forms called stalls, and meditate on things celestial, godly, angelical, divine. The famout picture of the "Light of the World" which hangs in Kebel College Chapel in the college of that name, attracts the more contemplative of folk, who sit in the small, Victorian side chapel, away from the hustle and bustle that is city life. There is the "Parks" where students play or punt on the river, the young feed the ducks while the old sit and watch or take their leisurely strolls. Aspects of Oxford today.

FIG. 4.2   Indented paragraph that can be used for patients with neglect dyslexia (see text for details).

purpose of the test was to make the layout of the text such that it was difficult for patients to form a compensatory "spatial strategy".

On the surface, the test appears to be a valuable screening measure, and also has potential as a retraining tool. However, a study by Towle and Lincoln (1991b) comparing errors made by 42 right hemisphere-damaged stroke subjects on this test against performance on text with straight margins and unpredictable text, found that both forms were equally capable of detecting mild neglect. Compared to performance on the star cancellation and article reading subtests of the BIT, the study found little clinical difference between various paragraph layouts. The results suggest that stroke subjects with left-sided neglect omit words whilst reading, whether or not the left-hand margin is indented. The reading task was sufficiently difficult for these subjects for varying the spatial layout to have little effect.

In contrast to Caplan's claim, there was little difference between the normal and indented paragraphs in detecting mild neglecters. Several subjects appeared to compensate for difficulties with the text by checking the meaning of what they read. If the text became meaningless, they re-read the relevant lines. This may be used as a compensatory strategy rather than using the margin as a guide when reading. Subjects with severe neglect appeared to have extreme difficulty on all reading tasks due to their erratic scanning patterns, and this group may be unable to control their scanning sufficiently to make use of the margin as a guide when reading. Differences may be seen between the texts if only those subjects with previously identified neglect are assessed.

In conclusion, Caplan's assertion that the indented paragraph test (IPT) is more sensitive to mild neglect than normally organised text was not supported by this study data. It is possible, however, that differences may be found if mild neglecters are assessed using this type of task. When using a cut-off of one or more omissions to indicate neglect, Caplan's IPT showed excellent agreement with normal text and good agreement with the double-indented paragraph. Both types of paragraphs were able to detect mild neglecters. Reading appears to be a difficult task for patients with neglect, and those who omit words when reading will do so on any reading task of sufficient length.

Generally, the two types of neglect dyslexia can be assessed reasonably well using existing reading materials in most clinical departments, although providing a patient with lists of words which may be somewhat more sensitive to neglect dyslexia may provide additional help in assessing whether the problem is present.

ASSESSMENT OF EXTINCTION

As mentioned in Chapter 1, extinction is a phenomenon that can be elicited by the clinician in auditory, visual, or tactile modalities. Extinction is defined as when a patient fails to detect a stimulus on the affected side when it is co-presented with a similar stimulus on the other side, despite the fact that the single stimulus on the affected side is usually easily detected. When testing extinction using bilateral simultaneous stimulation, it is useful to include interspersed unilateral stimuli.

The clinical significance of extinction remains unclear, however. There are many neglect patients who show no extinction and vice versa. In the clinical setting, evidence of extinction should not be used as evidence for neglect. Most methods for assessing visual, somatosensory, and auditory extinction are derived from clinical assessments more than a century old.

QUESTIONNAIRE MEASURES OF NEGLECT

Clinicians interested in a more functional approach to neglect, find it helpful to discover the types and frequency of everyday behaviours that have been affected by the patient's condition. Several questionnaires have been produced to assess the degree of functional impairment arising from neglect. The original standardisation of the BIT included a short checklist questionnaire (Halligan et al., 1991) that was completed by a relative/therapist for each patient.

Towle and Lincoln (1991a) published a questionnaire that attempted to measure patients subjective accounts of everyday activities in their own home and scores on this questionnaire correlated significantly with performance on the star cancellation test from the BIT. The most frequently reported problems for neglect subjects were feeling clumsy and misreading words. The authors argue that the questionnaire may be used in hospital as it may be a useful and easy way of identifying functional difficulties that such patients experience in their daily life.

Another questionnaire devised by Azouvi et al. (1996) has the advantage of having the same questions for both relatives and carers, thus allowing an estimate of the patient's anosognosia to be made. Many of the items on this questionnaire concern personal neglect. For instance, relatives or staff are asked to assess whether the patient:

(a) fails to shave or groom on the left side of the face;
(b) does not adjust clothing properly on the left side of the body;
(c) fails to clean the left side of the mouth after eating;
(d) fails to use or properly align the left arm or leg.

All the above questionnaires can be used to assess awareness of neglect on the part of the patient, by having staff or relatives complete them, as well as the patient. Patients with anosognosia for their neglect will tend to rate themselves as having fewer and less severe problems than the observers.

ASSESSMENT OF SUSTAINED ATTENTION

Up until now, we have been talking predominantly about lateralised aspects of the disorder, but in this section we will consider the influence that *non-lateralised* aspects of the disorder may make to neglect performance. A number of studies have shown a close connection between neglect and sustained attention, and indeed one has shown that neglect can be improved by training sustained attention (Robertson et al., 1995). It may be, therefore, important to assess sustained attention along with measures of neglect.

A quick way of assessing sustained attention is to use the Elevator Counting Task from The Test of Everyday Attention (Robertson, Ward, Ridgeway, & Nimmo-Smith, 1994b, 1996). Here, the subject is required to count a series of strings of tones which come at irregular intervals. This test is not arithmetically demanding, but requires the ability to maintain attention for up to 45 seconds at any one time. There is a much higher than normal failure on this test by patients with neglect.

Compared to right brain damaged patients without neglect who were matched on age, time post stroke and degree of left-sided hemiplegia, patients with visuospatial neglect were significantly more impaired on the Elevator Counting Test (Robertson, Manly, et al., 1997). Furthermore, there was a significant correlation between performance on this test of auditory sustained attention and all measures of visuospatial neglect.

A recent case of developmental neglect has also been reported in a 9-year-old boy. As would be predicted from what we know about neglect and sustained attention, this boy's lateralised problems were associated with severe deficits in sustained attention (Manly, Robertson, & Verity, 1997).

TROUBLESHOOTING

It is not uncommon for therapists to refer a patient for assessment for spatial neglect, only to find that the psychologist's assessment on formal tests showed little or no evidence of neglect. The therapist may be somewhat confused since they can see their patient catching fingers in wheelchair, failing to move the left leg during therapy, or knocking over the objects on the left during kitchen practice. How does one reconcile these apparent contradictions?

Clinical experience suggests four possible ways: namely confusion in terminology, varying sensitivity of formal tests, individual fluctuations in neglect performance, and test practice or familiarity with specific materials.

Confusions In terminology

As outlined in Chapter 1, a large number of different phenomena are currently used to describe neglect. It is important to point out, however, that the condition represents one of several different neurological and neuropsychological symptoms typically found after unilateral brain damage. Hence, there is always the danger that behaviours attributed to neglect will be misdiagnosed in favour of other sensory or motor impairments. A neurologist for instance, may discover the presence of somatosensory extinction, and may query the possibility of neglect being present. However, as already indicated, extinction can be present without neglect and vice versa. Similarly, the occupational therapist may find that the patient has failed to dress properly on the left side, and may refer the patient for further testing. The formal assessment will consist largely of visually based tests performed on the desktop. We know from Chapter 1 that neglect of the body (personal neglect) and neglect of external space do not necessarily go together, and one can frequently find cases where a patient suffers from one and not the other. So, the occupational therapist very correctly observed the presence of personal neglect, and the neuropsychologist very correctly reported the absence of a peripersonal or visual neglect. One therefore has to be precise about the behaviours one is referring to when talking about whether or not a particular patient has neglect.

Formal versus informal testing

It is a not an uncommon experience to find a patient, particularly one who has been in hospital for some time, to perform within normal limits on standardised tests of neglect, only to demonstrate neglect behaviours on the ward or at home. There are several possible reasons for this discrepancy. One is that most forms of clinical testing make the patient more attentive (albeit temporarily) to their environment and task demands. In short, the mere awareness that they are being tested is sometimes sufficient to make the patient more vigilant and, hence, to remind them to check to the left and continue to search the left side in the testing situation. Many cues associated with formal testing therefore, may serve to remind the patient to pay attention and to concentrate on what he or she is doing. These may help to implement compensatory strategies of scanning to the left which they may have learned during rehabilitation, but which they find difficult to implement in real life.

In their normal environment, such patients may not have such reminders. They are typically left to their own devices, particularly when occupied on some activity such as cooking a meal or making tea. These patients may well fail to remember to attend to the left or put effort into searching to the left, and hence there is the risk of accidents and other problems.

Fluctuations in neglect

As we outlined in Chapter 1, people with unilateral neglect commonly have great difficulty in sustaining attention over time. It may be that although they can remember to look to the left or compensate for the neglect in certain situations, they have great difficulty in spontaneously doing this when occupied by other things. Research has shown for instance, that neglect worsens if you give people mental arithmetic type tasks to do or even engage them in conversation. This is likely also to apply to more everyday activities such as planning a meal.

Fluctuations in neglect have also been attributed to fatigue, time of day, previous activities, patient learning, and compensation. For example, when John (Case 1, pp. 4–6) is assessed after his physiotherapy, late in the afternoon, he scores more poorly on several of the BIT tests than he does if they were administered early in the morning. If, as suggested, neglect and sustained attention are linked, then fluctuations in attention may be expected to influence neglect. Someone who is alert and aroused is likely to show less neglect in a particular situation than someone who is stressed or more tired, as one commonly encounters in right hemisphere brain damaged patients. Although some fluctuations in neglect performance can be expected, there are few studies that have formally evaluated neglect performance over the course of a day.

Levy, Blizzard, Halligan, and Stone (1995), examined 22 patients with acute stroke and 19 patients with convalescent stroke twice on the same day using the modified BIT referred to earlier. In contrast to many clinical accounts most of these patients failed to show significant fluctuations.

Practice effects

Over the course of recovery in hospital or rehabilitation centre, it is not uncommon to find a steady improvement in neglect, such that patients no longer show problems navigating, bumping into things, or having accidents. Although formal testing can confirm this, and patients are often discharged home in the belief that the neglect has fully recovered, it is quite common to find problems of neglect still arising outside the hospital environment when the patient is tired, distracted, or stressed, as described in Box 4.5.

BOX 4.5   Consequences of visual neglect in everyday life

Weinstein and Friedland (1977a) recount the case of the young man with mild neglect who having recovered from a ruptured aneurysm was asked to come down to the Bureau of Internal Revenue department to account for some unpaid income tax. Being understandably nervous, he was almost run over when he failed to notice a truck coming from his left while crossing the street on the way to the tax offices. Worse still inside the Bureau of Internal Revenue building, the man was almost arrested when he entered a ladies room after having misread the sign "WOMEN" as ". . MEN"!

One reason for this apparent recovery is that most neglect patients have derived a benefit from being tested and learning to scan to the left. We have already mentioned that formal testing is one such situation which reminds them to scan to the left, but other familiar situations can equally well acquire this ability to "prompt" attention to the left. One study by Lennon (1994), for instance, showed how a patient in the physiotherapy gymnasium frequently bumped into objects, but learned not to do so by being trained to search for red patches which were placed on all the normal collision points. This patient learned to scan for these red patches, so learned to avoid the collisions, and persisted in doing so even after the red patches were taken off. However, when the patient returned home, he continued to bump into corners and protrusions just as badly as he had done in the gymnasium prior to the therapy. The therapy had to be adjusted to the home setting, as the patient had only learned to scan to the left at particular points in the particular setting of the hospital gymnasium. This was highly specific learning, and produced no generalisation beyond that setting. So, less formally, patients can learn after a few painful collisions to go through the doorway correctly, and can learn after a few days of comments by nurses, that they must search their plate to make sure they are eating all the food.

All of these responses may, however, be more or less linked to a very specific situation and do not reflect a general improvement over all situations. In summary, therefore, informal reports of neglect in real life situations should be considered together with formal test results in diagnosing neglect. In the next chapter we turn to the rehabilitation of neglect.

CHAPTER FIVE

Recovery, variability, and early attempts to treat visual neglect

NATURAL RECOVERY

Relatively little is known about the changes in neglect over time and few studies have charted the natural history of neglect. Some researchers have found that neglect is commonly seen in the early stages after stroke, but resolves completely by 6 months. In fact, features of neglect can continue to be disruptive in patient's daily activities long after the apparent resolution of the more florid symptoms, as we saw in Chapter 1. One study of recovery of neglect after right stroke found that the median period of recovery for 50% of the patients was 9 weeks; by 12 weeks there was a 90% chance of recovery. An illustration of recovery in one right brain damaged patient can be seen in the case of performance on the BIT subtests shown in Fig. 5.1. Here, we can see that the patient recovery is different for each test.

One group study followed up 44 consecutive patients who suffered an acute hemispheric stroke (18 right hemisphere, 26 left hemisphere) at 3 days and 3 months post stroke. Figure 5.2 shows the remission rates for the two groups on line cancellation. Fifty-five percent of right hemisphere subjects showed neglect at 3 days, as did 42% of the left brain damaged subjects. By 3 months, the corresponding figures were 33% and 0, respectively. Hence, it would appear from this study that the incidence of right neglect is only slightly less than that of left neglect in the acute stages, but that recovery from right neglect is both more rapid and more complete.

The mechanisms underlying the recovery of neglect are still poorly understood, but may involve both intra- and interhemispheric processes. For

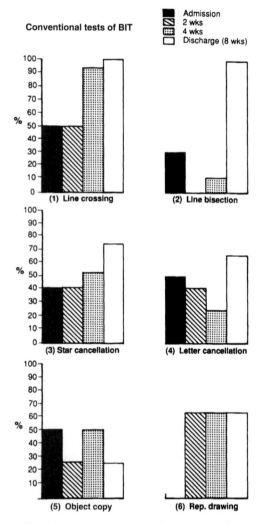

FIG. 5.1   Recovery of neglect on the BIT subtests. Percentage performance for each test over four time points.

example, it is possible that function is gradually restored as the damaged right hemisphere recovers (Herman, 1992). On the other hand, it is possible that the intact left hemisphere compensates by enhancing the reduced capabilities of the right hemisphere through inter-hemispheric connections.

Why is it that right brain damaged patients recover less frequently and less well from unilateral neglect than do left brain damaged patients? There are a number of possible reasons for this observation.

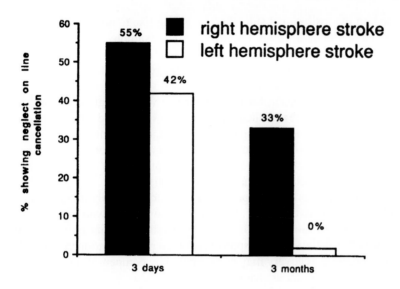

FIG. 5.2   Recovery rates for neglect after left and right damage (adapted from Stone et al., 1991).

One possible reason for the greater incidence of recovery of right compared to left neglect was suggested by Weintraub and Mesulam (1987), who argued that the right hemisphere is responsible for attending to both the left and right sides of space, while the left hemisphere only responds to the right half of space. According to this view, patients with left neglect do not recover so well, because their intact hemisphere can only attend to the right half of space, whereas right neglect patients, with an intact right hemisphere, can attend to both sides of space.

Another possible reason is that the right hemisphere is specialised for "global" processing of visual information, while the left hemisphere is responsible for "local" processing. This theoretical claim will be discussed in more detail later in this chapter. By global, one means a broad view of the visual world, as if the zoom lens of a camera were to be opened up wide. This type of perceptual processing is necessary in every day life as it provides a guide for the more local attentional processes. By local, it is meant a more restricted, detailed view of the parts of the scene or object, as if the zoom lens were focused in closely on one area.

Damage to the right hemisphere may lead to a reduction in global processing which is concerned with both the left and right visual fields. This reduction facilitates the more localised processing of the left hemisphere which is primarily concerned with right visual field (Robertson, 1992). As a result, the right brain damaged subjects show an increasing bias to attend to local stimuli located on the ipsilesional side, thereby giving rise to neglect of the left side (Halligan & Marshall, 1994). Figure 5.3 shows examples of this. Patients with right hemisphere damage managed to copy the 'local' small-scale elements of the figures, but could not copy the 'global' bigger-scale structure. The reverse was true for the left brain damaged subjects.

A third possible reason for the greater recovery of right compared to left neglect may be that the right hemisphere is also specialised for sustained attention and arousal, and that right brain damaged patients compensate less successfully because of poor general attention (see Chapter 3 for discussion of the assessment of sustained attention, and Chapter 6 for a description of rehabilitation methods related to sustained attention).

Many patients learn to compensate spontaneously for their neglect in ways which will be illustrated below. However, those patients who often have large right hemisphere lesions are more likely to also show deficits in sustained attention, as well as in the system responsible for orienting attention in space. As we saw in Chapter 2, recovery may be facilitated by compensation, which leaves the underlying disorder unchanged.

The findings of Goodale et al. (1990) suggest that, even after the apparent recovery of neglect, underlying distortions in spatial or attentional mechanisms may still exist. Researchers at Oxford (Campbell & Oxbury, 1976) assessing neglect on drawing task s up to 5 months post stroke came to a similar

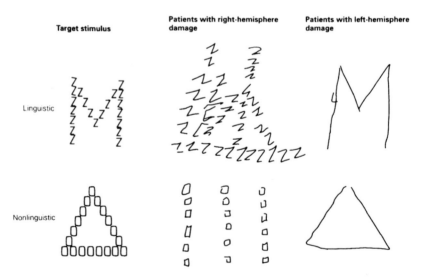

FIG. 5.3   Local versus global processing after left and right damage (see text for details). Reprinted from *Neuropsychologia*, *24*, Delis, D., et al. (1986), Hemispheric specialization of memory for visual hierarchical stimuli, 205–214, Copyright 1986, with permission of Elsevier Science.

conclusion using clinical drawing tests. They suggested that while the more florid features may resolve, many patients remained impaired on tests of spatial analysis and visual perception. It could be that Goodale et al.'s patients had learned to compensate for their neglect by compensatory visual control (see Chapter 2 for details of this argument).

If the underlying deficits are obscured by compensatory mechanisms, then it should be possible to elicit the basic deficit by presenting tasks which are made attentionally demanding or require a greater degree of spatial investigation. In other words, therapists should not be surprised if patients who appear to have recovered when observed in the quiet testing situation, may show neglect when tested under more taxing circumstances. This has been demonstrated experimentally by Robertson and Frasca (1992).

VARIABILITY IN NEGLECT PERFORMANCE

One of the most striking features of visual neglect that still continues to puzzle therapists and researchers is the fact that the condition is not an "all or none" phenomenon; in other words it is not unusual to see patients:

(a) who show neglect on one test but appear otherwise normal on another test;
(b) whose performance on the same test varies considerably over time; or
(c) who show neglect for one part of a test and not another.

An example of this first type of performance is described in Box 5.1 in the case of performance on line bisection and cancellation.

BOX 5.1   Dissociations between standard tests of visual neglect?

Six patients with unilateral right hemisphere damage were assessed on line bisection and cancellation—two of the most common clinical tests of visual neglect traditionally regarded as diagnostic for left (peripersonal) visuospatial neglect. Each patient performed both tasks. The results showed that two patients were unimpaired on both tasks, and two more impaired on both. The remaining two patients however showed a classic (and reliable) double-dissociation between the tasks. That is, one of the patients scored within normal limits on cancellation but was grossly impaired on bisection; another patient showed left-sided omissions on cancellation but was normal on line bisection. Halligan and Marshall (1992) argue that these results serve to question the validity of any single unitary concept of visuospatial neglect in peripersonal space.

The selective nature of neglect performance, however, can be seen in many everyday activities. Another example of this type of behaviour involves copying. Despite describing relevant features in a scene or picture presented to them, some patients may continue to draw or copy the right-hand side of an object that is left of another object, which in turn has also been drawn with the left side missing. This can be see in Fig. 5.4.

The puzzling thing is that patients who draw only one eye, arm, or leg to the right of the vertical axis of the configuration appear to "know" perfectly well that people have two eyes, arms, or legs. Similarly, when drawing a clock face, patients who only reproduce the numbers from 12 to 6 clearly "know" that a clock face has 12 numbers. Even more puzzling, is how some patients will place all 12 numerals along the right hemi-circumference of the clock face and yet insist in free vision that their reproduction looks fine when compared with that of a normal clock face.

A second and equally puzzling feature seen in many everyday examples of clinical neglect appears to be the patient's selective lack of awareness of spatial features on one task while being apparently aware of and making use of the same or very similar features on a slightly different version of the task. Bisiach and Rusconi (1990) and Young, Hellawell, and Welch (1992) describe patients with left neglect, who in the process of correctly tracing a line drawing of one

FIG. 5.4   Drawing showing neglect on the left side of both objects.

object pass over and through another object situated on the left side of the first, and yet appear not to notice the presence of the second object. A good example of this second type of performance is described in Box 5.2.

BOX 5.2   Dissociation between two forms of conscious perceptual awareness

Marshall and Halligan reported a new type of dissociation between two forms of conscious perceptual awareness in a patient with severe left neglect. When shown complex hierarchical drawings such as those in Fig. 5.5, in which a large (global) form (such as a geometric figure) was composed of smaller (local) forms (dots, circles, or letters) the patient reliably gave accurate verbal reports of the global structure. However, when required to cross out (i.e. cancel) the smaller subfigures (dots, circles, or letters) she could only cancel those on the right side of each global figure. In other words, conscious perception of the whole figure does not automatically lead to visual awareness of all the parts thereof. The results were interpreted by Marshall and Halligan (1995a) as showing that after right hemisphere damage the global perception of well-structured objects may remain intact even if attention cannot be automatically directed to local components on the left of a global figure.

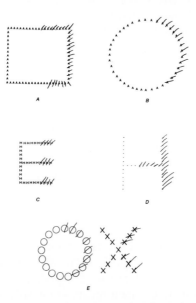

FIG. 5.5   Hierarchical drawings used to assess neglect. Reproduced with permission of Macmillan from Marshall, J.C., and Halligan, P.W., (1995). Seeing the forest but only half the trees. *Nature, 373*, 522. Copyright 1995, Macmillan Magazines Ltd.

EARLY ATTEMPTS TO REMEDIATE NEGLECT

In her review of neglect remediation, Lincoln (1991) suggests that as yet there is no well established treatment that has been satisfactorily demonstrated to be effective in the remediation of neglect disorders. While this conclusion is for the most part true, several attempts over the last 40 years have shown grounds for optimism.

As suggested by Calvanio, Levine, and Petrone (1993), there are two basic approaches to the treatment of perceptual disorders such as visual neglect. These are typically referred to as (a) impairment training or transfer of training; and (b) task-specific or functional training. The essential difference between the two approaches lies in the nature of the problem to be addressed. The transfer of training approach has as its basic assumption the belief that practice in a particular perceptual task will affect the patient's performance on similar perceptual tasks. Treatment begins by attempting to identify one or more of the primary impaired abilities that are thought to underlie the condition. Impairment-based training is similar to a program of physical fitness training whereby the training of strength, stamina, and speed through regular exercise is expected to benefit a wide variety of activities.

The functional approach on the other hand involves the repetitive practice of particular tasks, usually activities of daily living in the belief that it will make the patient more independent. The emphasis here is on treating the symptoms rather than the underlying problems.

The traditional approach to treating neglect has been and remains the transfer of training approach. Studies evaluating this approach are few and most generally indicate little significant benefit for the majority of patients (Lincoln, 1991).

Early attempts to rehabilitate neglect sprang from clinically based intuitions which considered the underlying impairment in behavioural terms, i.e. failing to look to the left. The aim of many of these remediation strategies was to facilitate natural recovery by increasing the patient's awareness of the condition; in particular, by attempting to reorient what many regarded as the main underlying problem, the patient's failure to orient automatically to their left side.

Scanning training

Visual neglect has been described as a disorder in "looking" rather than "seeing". Consequently early attempts to "treat" what most clinicians considered to be the underlying disorder focused on getting the patients to move their eyes (and head) and therefore their attention towards the affected side. The most obvious way to retrain patients who appear not to notice things on their left side after right brain damage is to remind them to scan or attend in that direction. This is the most commonly practised form of rehabilitation of neglect, the underlying principle of which is well illustrated by Fig. 5.6, which was drawn by the 7-year-old grandson of a stroke patient who showed neglect. The boy had visited his grandfather on several occasions and had, like his parents, observed that his grandfather was selectively ignoring people and objects located on the left side. The reasoning underlying this approach continues to form the major underlying rationale for most clinical attempts to rehabilitate neglect.

One of the earliest studies to remediate visual neglect was described by Lawson (1962), who tried a form of "scanning training". Lawson treated two cases of neglect by frequently reminding the patients to "look to the left", and also to use the fingers of their intact side to guide their vision while reading. They were also encouraged to find the centre of a book or food tray by using touch and then to use their finger position as a reference point from which to explore the page or tray systematically. Lawson concluded that although both patients improved on the tasks in which they were trained, they did not, however, get better on non-trained tasks. This finding (1962), raised the issue of generalisation central to all forms of rehabilitation carried out over the next 30 years. Nevertheless, in the 1970s and early 1980s, a series of important studies of scanning training were attempted by researchers in New York which subsequently became very influential.

FIG. 5.6   A 7-year-old's attempts to train his grandfather's neglect.

What is scanning training?

The basis for scanning training lies in behavioural psychology and learning theory. Behavioural approaches to learning emphasise the importance of linking particular stimuli with particular responses by repeatedly presenting the two together. The stimulus can then be connected to other stimuli, or even faded out in the hope that the responses in question become controlled by internal stimuli such as "look left" in the case of right brain damaged patients. The scanning training procedure developed by the New York group therefore tried to build up the habit of scanning left in a range of different situations. Some of the methods they used (e.g. Weinberg et al., 1977; Diller & Weinberg, 1977) included:

The scanning board.   In this treatment procedure, patients sat in front of a large wide board with a range of lights located on its periphery and in the middle (see Fig. 5.7). Patients were then required to point to those lights which they saw and to follow them with their eyes as successive lights were systematically turned on. In the first stages of training, lights were only illuminated on the right side of the panel, then, gradually, more and more lights towards the left were involved, and patients with neglect were gradually induced to make more

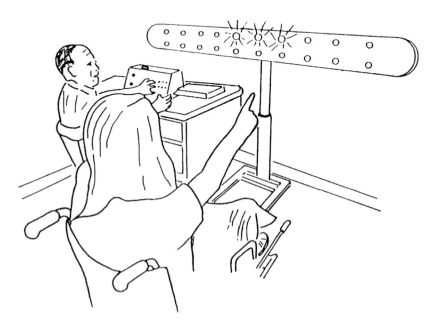

FIG. 5.7   Scanning board used in the training of visual neglect at the New York medical centre.

and more leftward eye movements further and further into the left visual field. Subjects were also encouraged to try and verbally control leftward movements by phrases such as "look left!", with the intention that they would learn voluntarily to look to the left in the range of situations without having to be reminded.

Reading training and end anchoring.   This technique of the New York group focused on the subjects' ability to read a full length of text in books and newspapers. The therapy involved placing a thick red "anchor line" in red ink or paper down the left side of any text. The patient was then required to read the text slowly line by line. The patient was not allowed to read a line until he or she had found the red anchor line on the left side in the visual field. To ensure that they had reached the far left of the line, it was emphasised they had to find a red anchor bar.

As training progressed, the width of the anchor bar was gradually reduced, so that it became less and less obvious. Eventually, it was faded out altogether, and in the meantime the patients had learned to find the left margin of the text before reading each line. In addition to the anchoring procedure, the New York researchers also used a line numbering method. Each line of text was numbered on the left side in a set order and patients were encouraged to regulate the line they were reading, by following the numerical sequence. This was done to reduce the tendency to skip lines, which many neglect patients do, in addition to the left neglect.

Finally, the training procedure also involved very low density and large print text. The density of the text was gradually increased until it approximated to normal newspaper format. The reason for doing this was that neglect is known to be more severe where the visual field is more densely packed with information.

Problems of generalisation

A number of researchers have attempted to evaluate the effectiveness of the scanning training approach, in order to see if it extended to real life applications, for example, training patients to scan using the scanning board while simultaneously navigating wheelchairs. Webster et al. (1984), suggested that while training on the scanning board showed improvements, they tended to be specific to the scanning board. In other words, it did not produce improvements on tasks such as reading or letter cancellation. Similarly, training in the anchoring procedures of the cancellation and reading tasks had little effect on scanning board performance.

These findings have been confirmed in a recent series of studies carried out in Holland. Using a multistage design involving scanning and reading training, with intervention phases of a fixed duration of 2 weeks, Wagenaar et al. (1992)

assessed the effects of scanning training. Three times in each intervention phase, performance was measured using a computerised visual scanning test, a line bisection test, and a letter cancellation test. In addition, wheelchair navigation was also assessed. Four out of the five patients showed a significant effect of visual scanning training on visual scanning behaviour, however, the effect remained restricted to the task on which it was specifically trained. The authors conclude that there was no evidence for any transfer of visual scanning training effects to other functional domains.

Ross (1992) examined the effects of computer-assisted visual scanning in the retraining of a functional scanning deficit in three patients using single subject designs. Computer-based intervention occurred after 2 to 3 weeks of baseline data and consisted of six to nine sessions of 15 to 30 minutes therapy spaced over 3 weeks. Post treatment baselines were collected over the following 2 weeks, including some on a functional scanning task. No significant change in performance on the functional task were found, confirming that computer intervention did not significantly affect performance on the functional task. The clinical significance of the results suggest that software-assisted remediation may not be an appropriate means of therapy for neglect.

Fanthome, Lincoln, Drummond, and Walker (1995) investigated the transfer of training approach using a variety of strategies including scanning. Fourteen patients with visual neglect identified on the BIT were involved. All patients received practice for 4 weeks on perceptual tasks designed to improve visual neglect and then results were analysed as single cases using an AB design. Only 3 of 14 patients completing the study showed improved perceptual test scores following treatment. These authors concluded that the transfer of training approach did not appear to enhance the recovery of most patients with visual neglect, although those with severe problems showed some improvement. Research in Rome (Antonucci et al., 1995) found that intensive implementation of procedures (24 1-hour treatment sessions over 2 months combined with opto-kinetic stimulation (see Chapter 6), produced significant improvements on several standard outcome tests of hemineglect. However, generalisation to situations in daily life at follow up several months later was not demonstrated. Also in Italy, Ladavas and colleagues (Ladavas, Menghini, & Umilta, 1994) reported improvements involving a scanning-based training regime, without clear evidence of generalisation.

The value of scanning training

The fact that most scanning training procedures produce negative results is in part predictable from the behavioural models in which they were based. Behavioural psychology emphasises the linkage of particular stimuli with *particular* responses, and do not explicitly provide for the training of more abstract and general functional skills which can be applied to non-trained situations. What appears to have occurred in the scanning training studies is that patients were successfully trained to scan to the left in particular situations, but generalised improvement seldom occurred.

Although generalisation to more functional situations has not (typically) been found, there is, however, some therapeutic benefit to be derived from this form of training. Patients can be trained to scan to the left while reading, for instance (and hence improve their enjoyment and retention of reading material), while eating, while washing, or while engaged in a range of other important activities. Therefore, it is possible that specific functional training may result in functional improvements.

The main limitations of the New York studies have been discussed by Lincoln (1991) and Robertson (1993). In her review of treatments for visual perceptual disorders, Lincoln points to the lack of relevance of the outcome measure, the fact that treatment procedures in the control group were ill-defined, and that the early studies consisted of group comparisons not determined by random allocation. Lincoln also argues that if treatments are to be of clinical value, one would expect them to produce higher levels of independence in activities of daily living or a decrease in time in hospital. The New York studies, evaluated outcome on tasks very similar to those being trained, using only descriptions to suggest that these changes had some practical significance for daily functional abilities.

The limitations of the New York-based studies and their replications can be turned into a virtue in those studies where specific aspects of the patients behaviour relevant to their particular functional recovery can be targeted. In other words, scanning training may be of limited use in producing specific responses (compensatory saccades) in specific situations (for example reading/writing tasks). Such improvements are of fundamental importance to the rehabilitation of individuals, given the importance of reading and writing in everyday life. A few subsequent studies have scaled down the ambitious aims of Diller and his colleagues and contented themselves with inducing specific response changes to specific stimuli, without aiming to produce generalised and spontaneously initiated changes in scanning behaviour.

One example is a Belgian study (Seron, Deloche, & Coyette, 1989) that used scanning methods in the case of a severe neglect patient, but failed to produce significant improvements. They also attempted self-instructional training, which also failed. However, their final attempt at therapy was successful in reducing the handicapping effects of neglect on the patient's everyday life. The treatment involved a "mental prosthesis", namely a device the size of a cigarette packet which gave a high-pitched buzz at random intervals between 5 and 20 seconds. This was placed in the patient's left shirt pocket, and he was encouraged to explore space to find the machine and switch it off. The result was a significant improvement in everyday functioning, where none had been obtained by the previous methods.

Another study (Robertson & Cashman, 1991) reported a 29-year-old woman with left sensory loss and visual neglect in the context of frontal lobe difficulties who presented problems in physiotherapy because she walked with her left foot heel-up in a highly unstable plantarflex position. She completely failed to learn to lower her heel on walking in spite of the fact that she could lower her heel to the floor on command. This could have led to an ankle injury.

A pressure-sensitive switch attached to a buzzer on her belt was inserted under her left heel, and a walking programme instituted. Time of heel contact during a 4-m walking test was gradually increased through a process of charting progress and setting goals. Improvements in her walking were recorded. These appeared to generalise to everyday life.

As reported in the previous chapter, Lennon (1994) showed how a patient with severe left neglect was trained to avoid collisions in the physiotherapy gymnasium by placing large coloured paper markers on the edges (of tables, corners, etc.) with which he habitually collided. This method is analogous to Weinberg et al.'s anchoring procedure for reading. The patient was trained to look for these markers, which he learned to do, and also to skirt round the obstacles with which he habitually collided. This he also learned. Once the markers were removed, the improved behaviour was maintained, though it did not generalise beyond the precise topography of the gymnasium and its furniture.

When the patient went home, he made as many collisions as before in the new environment. The procedure was therefore repeated in the home, with markers being placed on the edges with which he habitually collided. The treatment worked as before, and the effects persisted after removal of the paper markers. However, the behaviour change was again limited to the precise topography of his home and there was no further generalisation.

In summary, the above series of cases illustrate the potential remediability of specific responses to specific stimuli. But the conclusions of the previous section still hold, namely that time-efficient generalised scanning improvements in unilateral neglect as a result of training remain to be proved.

IMPLICATIONS FOR REHABILITATION

As we saw earlier, the main approach to usual neglect treatment in the late 1970s and 1980s was based on the assumption that the patient with neglect had lost the ability to focally attend automatically to the affected side unless explicitly requested or cued to do so (Riddoch & Humphreys, 1983). Hence, the main approach taken was one based on what appeared to be common sense; it was important to cue focal attention over to the neglected side.

From a rehabilitation point of view this approach has two major problems.

1. *The time-limited effect of therapist-dependent cueing.* The variable presentation of neglect between tests has implications for rehabilitation. For example, it is well known that left-sided cueing, the basic principle underlying most attempts to remediate neglect (including visual scanning) is often variable and transitory. It is, however, usually possible to direct a patient's attention to stimuli that they might otherwise spontaneously ignore by providing appropriate instructions and physical cues. Despite this many patients continue to ignore stimuli on the affected side.

The variability and short-terms effects of cueing in the case of line bisection is described in Box 5.3.

BOX 5.3   The temporal effects of left-sided cueing

What is crucial for rehabilitation is to know how long the improvement that results from cueing the patient will last. Can the patient's marking of the left end of a stimulus as in line bisection be maintained if a delay is imposed between marking the end of the line and bisection? In 1992, Halligan, Donegan, and Marshall evaluated the effect of three different temporal conditions against a standard condition of no temporal delay. This experiment was conducted using stimulus lines of 180mm that were presented in blocks of 10 trials; blocks in each of the conditions were repeated with conditions pseudo-randomised. The conditions were as follows.

(1)   Standard condition (no cueing) (×6 blocks).
(2)   The patient marks the left end of the line with a small cross and then immediately bisects the line (×4 blocks).
(3)   This condition differs from condition 2 (above) in that a delay of 5 seconds is imposed between marking the left end of the line and bisecting it. After marking the left end, the patient removes his arm from the left end of the line, places it on his lap, and is instructed to look away from the line until the experimenter tells him to bisect the line (×3 blocks).
(4)   This condition is equivalent to condition 3, except that the delay is increased to 10 seconds (×3 blocks).

The standard condition (zero delay) showed a consistent deviation of 46.9mm to the right of centre. With short delays (5 or 10 seconds) between left end marking and bisection, performance rapidly deteriorated; the results of the 10-second delay begins to approach the extreme right-sided bias of the standard condition. In other words, whatever "activation" effect is provoked by this cueing, it appeared to dissipate quickly. The results confirm the pessimistic view that passive cueing, although producing short-term improvements of neglect, produce no long-term carry-over of improvement once the manipulations involved are withdrawn. Figure 5.8 shows the short-term effects of cueing. In this case, the patient marked the left end of the line just before bisection (A). Although bisection performance improves, it rapidly falls off when the same lines without cues are presented (B).

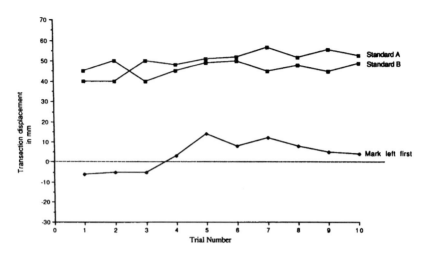

FIG. 5.8   Short-term effects of scanning on line bisection. Reprinted with permission of Psychology Press Limted, Hove, UK from Halligan, P.W., Donegan, C.A., Marshall, J.C. (1992). When is a cue not a cue? On the intractability of visuospatial neglect. *Neuropsychological Rehabilitation*, *2*, 283–293.

2. *The approach requires the patient to be made initially aware of the stimulus on the neglected side.* In addition to the test materials, treatment invariably requires the involvement of an additional dynamic cue—usually in the form of the therapist or an alerting device to direct attention initially to the physical cue. In other words, left-sided cues are often not useful in themselves, without the additional involvement of directional cues which points them out in the first place. If most treatment procedures are to be successful, they are largely dependent on the ability of the patient to learn to self-cue in situations outside the framework of the specific training

The problem therefore from a rehabilitation point of view lies in having to make the patient initially aware of the stimuli on their neglected side. Most previous accounts exclusively emphasise the redirection of voluntary attention. This in turn requires the input of an additional cue.

What would be useful therefore is an intervention or strategy that could operate as an automatic or data-driven orientation cue. In the early 1990's, several studies investigating the global and local properties of tests suggested that it may be possible to derive improved performance by changing particular features of a task or the specific demands of the test. One of the first examples concerned performance on a cancellation task described in more detail in Box 5.4.

The data outlined in Box 5.4 suggested that, depending on the specific task demands, it was possible for some severe neglect patients to use information

BOX 5.4   Homing in on neglect

This simple experiment, reported by Halligan and Marshall (1993a), has four separate steps. Each step includes the requirement to cancel all the targets of the line crossing test from the BIT (Halligan et al., 1991). The *first* step (standard condition) required the patient to cross out all the target lines seen on the page. The *second* step was the same as the first, except that immediately prior to the start of the task, the patient was asked to mark each corner of the stimulus page with a cross. The *third* step was the same as the first, except that this time the patient was asked to indicate the corners of the stimulus page after he had completed crossing out all the lines he could see on the page. The *fourth* step was identical to the first step. The idea behind the experiment was that if the two intermediary steps (2 and 3) had any effect, the fourth step would show whether or not there was any beneficial carry-over effect on performance. Omission scores from the four presentations of line crossing were calculated. In each of the four conditions the patient failed to cross out all the target lines located on the left side of the stimulus page. In steps 2 and 3, however, the patient showed no difficulty in locating and marking the four corners of the stimulus page. The results make clear that the patients apparent awareness of the spatial extent of the A4 stimulus page made no difference to his cancellation of the targets contained within the area whose corners he had accurately indicated.

from global processing. There is some evidence that normal individuals can modify global/local processing voluntarily. The principle impairment of global processing after right hemisphere damage, however, resides in the fact that it cannot automatically direct focal attention leftward when a local operation is required in that spatial area. When specifically required to deploy global attention to the stimulus configuration as a whole, the damaged right hemisphere can do so to some extent, but the intact left hemisphere drives focal attention rightwards as soon as the local task of cancellation is engaged (Halligan & Marshall, 1994a).

These different pieces of evidence suggest that although the attentional spotlight may be impaired and skewed to the ipsilesional side on most tasks that demand focal processing such as cancellation or bisection, it is still possible to activate the damaged right hemisphere by selectively cueing within the ipsilesional field or by specific instructions. Evidence in favour of this hypothesis was first described by Marshall and Halligan (1991a) in a study that compared bisection performance on squares and lines. Box 5.5 describes this study.

On the basis of the findings described in Box 5.5 and other data, Halligan and Marshall (1991a) concluded that particular features of the task were facilitating a change in the size of the *attentional spotlight* (in this case, the vertical length of the figure on the right side). The simple explanation for this result is as

BOX 5.5   Line versus square bisection

Halligan and Marshall (1991a) described a patient with severe left visuospatial neglect following right hemisphere stroke using a modified line bisection task. In the first part of their study they showed that while the patient bisected horizontal lines significantly to the right of true centre, he was extremely accurate in placing a mark at the centre of an equivalent outlined square. The authors showed that the accuracy obtained when bisecting the square task could not have been derived from calculating vertical (radial) line bisection. The experiment showed that the individual horizontal lines of the square could be bisected significantly more accurately than the same lines presented without the square. A final experiment showed that the crucial figural component for the accurate estimation of the lateral extent in the case the square was the large vertical (radial) line located in *right* space. The results whereby a square of similar lateral extent to that of a line was bisected significantly more accurately is consistent with a model in which a large, global stimulus in right space engages and enhances the lesioned right hemisphere's intrinsic capacity to deploy global attention.

follows; after right brain damage focal process are skewed to the ipsilesional side on most tasks that explicitly require focal processing such as line crossing, cancellation, drawing, and line bisection. However, it is possible that the damaged right hemisphere can be selectively activated in some patients by the use of specific cues situated within the *ipsilesional* field.

Studies by Halligan and Marshall (1994b), that set out to evaluate which specific features of the square figure were contributing to global processing found that the vertical extents of the figure were significant. If global attention could be engaged by the vertical dimension of the figures (which seemed likely on the basis of the previous data), then, although highly counter-intuitive, it may be possible for a right-sided cue (which the patient should have little difficulty in attending to) to improve left neglect performance on a traditional test such as line bisection. A description of this experiment is provided in Box 5.6.

The results described in Box 5.6 have implications for the remediation of neglect. If global processing can be activated in some patients then it may be possible to attract selective attention to relevant features of the task located on the left. If the guiding structure provided by a global scale is no longer available then it is difficult to direct local attention from the left. Once attention has been focused in this fashion the global view may be lost to conscious awareness and the patient no longer sees any reason to explore leftwards.

The suggestion is that in left visuospatial neglect, global processing can remain intact to a significant degree in some patients. In most cases, this global processing of the visual world can no longer be used to direct automatic focal attention to objects and parts of objects that require further local analysis.

BOX 5.6   Right cueing for left neglect

In this study Halligan and Marshall (1994c) report three cases of left visuospatial neglect after right hemisphere injury. In the first experiment, the three patients, who all showed significant impairment on horizontal line bisection, showed themselves to be differentially sensitive to "focal" left-sided cueing. All three, however, were considerably more accurate when requested to mark the centre of squares whose horizontal extent was identical to that of the previously employed lines. In a second experiment, two of the three patients showed significant improvements on horizontal line bisection when a thin vertical line was positioned at the right end of the horizontal line. In the third experiment, Halligan and Marshall showed that the extent of improvement using the right-sided line was positively related to the total length of the vertical line in right space. The authors argue in conclusion that cueing with a large vertical configuration in right space can serve to increase the diameter of the "attentional spotlight" within which the stimulus configuration is perceived.

Without this ability, local attention which is biased to the right will always represent too little of the visual world.

We are only aware of the absence of information if we focus attention on the relevant sensory domain and find nothing there. When attention is perpetually focused right then the patient is in no position to observe the absence of left-sided input. Even if selective attention can be voluntarily moved leftward, the necessary guiding framework provided by a global scale is no longer available. Consequently, the patient no longer sees any reason to continue to explore leftwards.

CONCLUSIONS

(1) Remedial training of neglect by leftward scanning remains intrinsically unstable and short lived.

(2) The variable size of an "attentional spotlight" may be influenced by the task demands involved. In other words, stimulus manipulation may activate the damaged or impaired right hemisphere, thereby increasing the attentional spotlight and therefore overcoming the left hemisphere's tendency to deploy focal attention rightwards.

(3) With respect to the remediation of visual neglect using external cueing techniques, it is too early to draw any firm conclusions. However, it would appear that these are promising lines of research deserving further investigation to see if lasting functional effects can be obtained.

CHAPTER SIX

Different attempts to treat visual neglect

INTRODUCTION

In the light of the somewhat disappointing results of scanning training, described in Chapter 5, the question arises as to what other rehabilitation attempts might improve neglect? Many forms of neglect intervention attempt to activate the brain on the affected side, with the intention of improving the patient's ability to attend to the affected side. In this chapter, we consider a number of different approaches, some of which have been tested clinically, and others which although (as yet) unproven may nevertheless be of potential value.

LIMB ACTIVATION TREATMENTS

Most patients with severe (left) neglect present with a motor paralysis that prevents them using the left hand. As a result, most paper and pencil tests to assess neglect use the right hand, which is primarily under the control of the intact left hemisphere. Since we know (from anatomy and functional imaging studies) that use of the right hand activates the left hemisphere, it may also be the case that use of the right hand may in fact be contributing to neglect performance. In other words, left neglect may be regarded as resulting more from the contribution of the intact left hemisphere given impairment to the right hemisphere. On perceptual motor tasks such as line bisection and cancellation, the non-lesioned left hemisphere may be more activated relative to the damaged right hemisphere. In other words, some of neglect performances observed in patients with neglect may be due to the selective involvement of the non-damaged left hemisphere as it is no longer inhibited by an the underactive right hemisphere (Kinsbourne, 1993).

The question, therefore, arises as to what would happen if the patient with visual neglect could use the affected side when performing assessments and carrying out everyday tasks? The illustration in Fig. 6.1 shows the result in one patient. The flower on the left in Fig. 6.1 was drawn with the right hand by a man with left-sided neglect whose left hand was not paralysed. The flower on the right was drawn by the same man (minutes later), using his left hand. This performance suggests that the side of the body controlled by the neurologically impaired right hemisphere was capable, when not paralysed, of carrying out the drawing task without neglect. It is possible that using the left hand cues attention to the left side of space.

There are now a number of studies that have found similar results on cancellation and line bisection tasks. For instance, when asked to search and cross out from a complex array of shapes and figures, neglect patients who use their left arm found significantly more targets than patients who use their right arm.

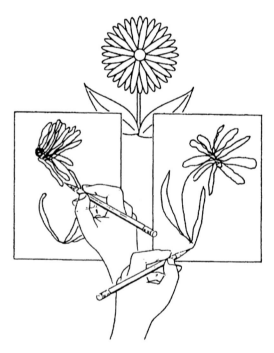

FIG. 6.1   Illustration of how using the hand controlled by the damaged right hemisphere can result in reduced neglect for the left side of an object.

Halligan and Marshall (1989a) reported such a patient who after a right hemisphere stroke could use his left hand. Despite severe left-sided neglect, he bisected lines more accurately and cancelled more left-sided targets on star cancellation when permitted to use his left hand.

Use of the left hand "activated" the impaired right hemisphere and subsequently reduced his neglect (see Robertson and North, 1992). Another interpretation is that doing something on the left side of space, such as moving the left hand, draws attention to that side and consequently this 'cueing' procedure may help reduce neglect over and above any hemispheric activation benefit derived from simply using the left hand itself. A study by Halligan, Manning and Marshall (1990a) supports this idea: their patient was asked to bisect lines using the right hand followed by the left hand. There was significantly less neglect when the left hand was used, but this advantage was subsequently abolished when the left hand was positioned on the right side of the line before the patient bisected it. In other words, if attention was first attracted to the right side, the advantage of using the left hand disappeared.

Other studies, however, suggested beneficial effects when moving the left hand on the left side of space in those patients who have some movement in the left hand (Robertson & North, 1992). Since attention is directed both to the left side of the body as well as to the left side of external space during such movements, the effect is to produce a more powerful cueing or activation of the brain's representations for that side of space.

Practical Implications For Rehabilitation

In describing the scanning training in Chapter 4, we reported how previous studies had often used the paralysed left arm as a "perceptual anchor" for training the patient to scan to the left. If patients can also move the left arm (however little), then one may get the combined effect of placing the left arm at the border of any activity if it is moved partially under voluntary control into position. Several case studies have now shown that improvements in daily life can be obtained by training patients to generate even quite modest movements with their partially paralysed left side of their body when performing everyday activities (Robertson, North, & Geggie, 1992).

Figure 6.2 shows the changes in star cancellation between a baseline to a post-training period. ADL ratings showed comparable improvements. This training was done by means of a "neglect alert device", a simple electronic box attached to the patient's trouser belt, with two switches attached to different parts of the left side of the patient's body. The "neglect alert device" was programmed to *buzz* at certain intervals, and whenever it did, the patient was encouraged to manually press whichever switch was illuminated in order to stop the buzzing. This was done during different activities and therapies, and was simply a means of trying to train the person to *activate* the left side of the

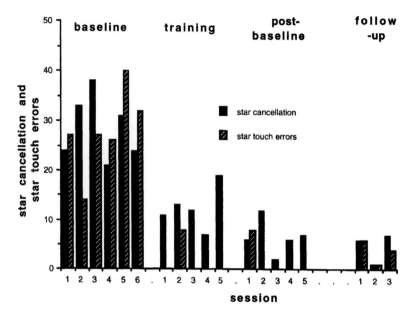

FIG. 6.2   Improvements in neglect as a result of limb activation training. Robertson, I.H., North, N., and Geggie, C. (1992). *Journal of Neurology, Neurosurgery and Psychiatry, 55,* 799–805. (Reproduced with permission of the BMJ Publishing Group, London).

body. In a study evaluating the "neglect alert device" (Robertson et al., 1998) several functional measures were used, including positioning of the body when walking through a series of corridors and doorways, the extent to which the left side was attended to during hair combing, and the positioning of a series of "buns" on a mock "baking tray". In this latter task, devised in Sweden (Tham & Tegner, 1996), patients are given sixteen blocks of wood and are told to position them on a large board so that they are symmetrically laid out as if they are "buns on a baking tray" to be placed in an oven. Patients with neglect tend to cluster the "buns" to the right-hand side. Like most clinical tests of neglect, this is a complex perceptuo-motor task and impaired performance can be caused by other factors in addition to neglect.

Figures 6.3, 6.4, and 6.5 show patient performance on three measures over lengthy baseline, treatment, and follow-up periods. It can be seen from these figures, that all three functional measures improved as a result of training (none of which were carried out during the test sessions). Terminating the use of the "neglect alert device" coincided with a decline in the improvements in two of the three measures. However, one of the measures, the baking tray test, did maintain improvement despite the cessation of training over a long period. The reasons for this are as yet unclear.

Hair combing right bias

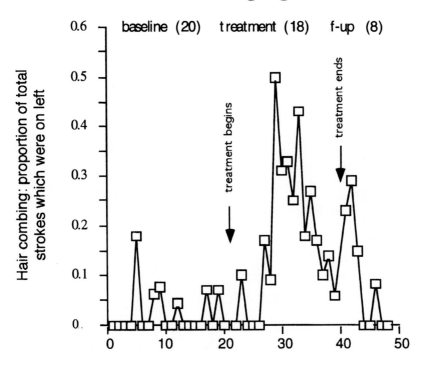

FIG. 6.3   Improvements in self care (hair combing) as a result of limb activation training.

Studies by Robertson and North (1994) found that the benefit of activating the left arm was negated if the two limbs were moved simultaneously. This can be interpreted as a form of "motor extinction", whereby the beneficial cueing or activation effects of the left hand movements (right hemisphere) were cancelled by the stronger cueing and activation of moving the right hand (left hemisphere). This study, furthermore, has implications for how patients with neglect should be treated in therapy; such patients should preferentially benefit from unilateral activation of their hemiplegic side.

This view is compatible with the results of another study showing that in non-neglecting hemiplegic patients more than a year post stroke, significant improvements in the function of the hemiplegic arm were obtained when the patients were preventing from using the non-hemiplegic limb for extended periods (Taub et al., 1993). These improvements persisted long after the intervention ended, and suggest that latent activation of the damaged hemisphere

Body Positioning

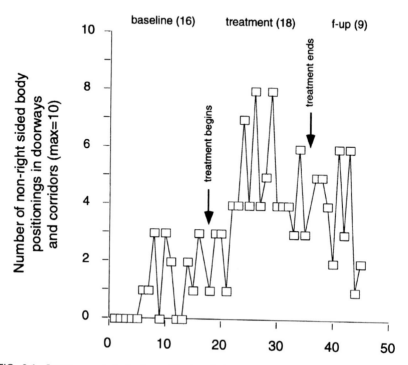

FIG. 6.4   Improvements in body positioning during walking as a result of limb activation training.

may be inhibited by activation of the undamaged hemisphere, again emphasising the value of some degree of unilateral, as opposed to bilateral, activation.

AUDITORY FEEDBACK

Several different types of auditory stimulation have been used in attempts to modify and reduce neglect. These vary between studies employing explicit feedback to those that have used different types of music as a way of activating the damaged right hemisphere. The most common form of auditory feedback that has been used to reduce neglect can be seen in most rehabilitation or hospital wards; therapist and nurses remind patients to look left when they fail to find what they are looking for or where they are going to. The approach has been evaluated more systematically in the case of eye movements.

Block ("buns") positioning

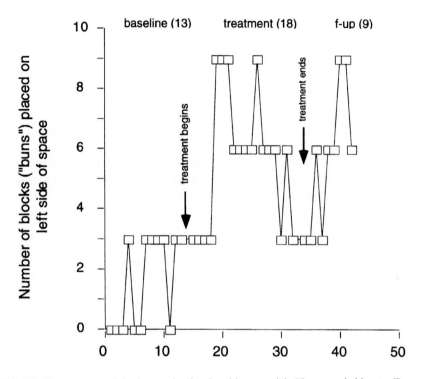

FIG. 6.5   Improvements in laying out simulated cooking materials ("buns on a baking tray") as a result of limb activation training.

It is a well-established clinical observation that patients with visual neglect tend not to direct their eyes to the visual field contralateral to their stroke. Using eye monitoring equipment, Ishiai et al. (1987) have shown that patients with visual field deficits, unlike patients with neglect, often employed compensatory strategies for looking to their affected side. Although neglect patients often fail to move their eyes spontaneously over to the left with feedback, it might be possible to reduce neglect if they were given information as to where their eyes were looking.

To evaluate whether feedback of eye movements might be a potential treatment strategy, Fanthome et al. (1995) employed a randomised control trial that compared knowledge of eye movements contigent upon auditory feedback. The treatment group ($n = 9$) was seen for over 2 hours a week for 4 weeks. Eye movement detection glasses provided an auditory signal in the form of a continuous bleep as a reminder if and when the patient failed to move their eyes to the left after a fixed interval of 15s. The control group of ($n = 9$) patients received no treatment for their neglect. Comparison of the two groups at 4 weeks and then a further 4 weeks later showed no significant difference either in eye movements or neglect performance as measured on the BIT.

TRUNK ROTATION

One aspect of neglect performance that is often taken for granted by therapists and clinicians, as we saw in Chapter 1, remains the question of which "reference frame" is involved when describing "left" neglect. In other words, what is neglect "left" of? The midline of the body has been shown to be one of the major frames of reference that determines the relative extent of "left" neglect. Many studies have shown that visual stimuli falling to the left or right of the body midline can determine whether or not they are detected.

A study by Karnath, Schenkel, and Fischer (1991) in Germany showed for instance that simply rotating the trunk 15° to the left could significantly reduce left neglect in a way that neither rotating the eyes or the head produced. When the trunk is rotated by 15° to the left, (while the head and eyes are fixed straight ahead) visual stimuli on the left of the midline defined by the head and eyes are actually located spatially to the *right* of the midline defined by the rotated body. Figure 6.6 shows where visual stimuli are located with the body straight ahead and the body rotated 15° to the left.

More recently, French researchers (Wiart et al., 1995) devised an ingenious method to combine the scanning training methods used by Diller in the New York studies (mentioned in Chapter 5) and trunk rotation. They fixed a metal frame to the patient's trunk and suspended a long pointer that was fixed to this frame over the patient's head. Patients had then to engage in visual search tasks of the type used by Diller. Instead of using their eyes or fingers, they had to use movements of the trunk to move the long pointer and to detect and touch targets on a large screen in front of the patient. The results of this study showed significant and long-lasting improvements in unilateral neglect during training with some evidence of generalisation to functional tasks. This is an example of a very interesting development which combines theoretically important ideas with clinically relevant methods such as scanning training.

SUSTAINED ATTENTION TRAINING

Sustained attention refers to the ability to maintain alertness in circumstances where there is little change or novelty in the environment. While a loud noise or unexpected visual object draws our attention from the outside (that is *exogenously*), we also need the additional capacity to maintain attention (that is

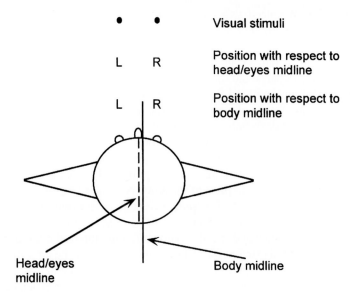

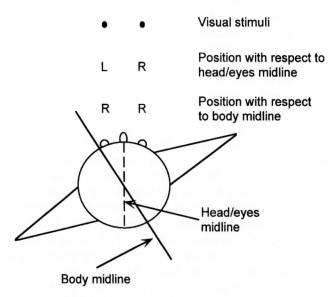

FIG. 6.6   Importance of the body midline in determining the relative "leftness" and "rightness" of visual stimuli (see text for details).

endogenously). We need this capacity when driving along a straight and unchanging road at night, when listening to a long lecture, or reading a long chapter.

The ability to sustain a state of alertness is strongly represented in the right hemisphere, and in particular the right frontal lobe. This has been shown in the study investigating the blood flow changes that take place when subjects are required to sustain a state of alertness (Pardo, Fox, & Raichle, 1991). Subjects were asked to count the number of times they were touched on their feet over a 40-second period while their regional cerebral blood flow was charted using PET (positron emission tomography). Irrespective of which toe was stimulated, the right fronto-parietal areas were significantly more activated in this task of sustained attention to parts of the body. A similar finding was obtained when subjects had to look at a computer screen to detect brief dimmings of a central stimulus (Pardo et al., 1991).

Posner (1993) argues that the ability to shift attention to the left or right is controlled by a spatial orientation system, partly located in the inferior parietal lobes of the brain (see Chapter 2). This is one of the areas thought to be impaired in spatial neglect. A second attention system modulates the efficiency with which this spatial orientation system works; this is the right hemisphere sustained attention system described earlier. Posner argues that the sustained attention system has particularly close links with the neurotransmitter norepinephrine, and that there is evidence that the norepinephrine pathways are more strongly represented in the right as compared to the left hemisphere. However, since the strongest endpoints of this neurotransmitter system are close to the location of the spatial orientation system, the effects of increasing sustained attention may therefore provide a secondary modulation of the primary orientation system. If this is so, then this modulation may provide yet another approach for reducing neglect that bypasses the problems associated with lack of awareness so characteristic of neglect (see Chapter 2). An impairment of sustained attention can be manifested in the tendency to lose concentration easily during therapy. Relatives often comment that the stroke patient "drifts off" and appears not to be listening to them while they are talking with them. Impairments of sustained attention can be assessed using tasks such as the Elevator Counting Task from The Test of Everyday Attention (see Chapter 4). In this test, patients have to count a series of tones while imagining that they are standing in an elevator, with each tone representing a different floor; the task is to count the number of tones and state the floor eventually arrived at.

Could lateralised neglect performance be improved by directing treatment resources to the sustained attention systems? The first evidence in non-neglect patients that suggested this possibility was carried out in Canada by Meichenbaum and Goodman (1971), with impulsive children. Their studies showed that attention could be brought under voluntary control by "self-instructional" procedures. The results suggest that it may be possible to train neglect patients who also had sustained attention problems to improve alertness by training them to (self-endogenously) "switch up" their sustained attention system using the types of learned verbal self-instructions used by Meichenbaum and Goodwin. If Posner's account is correct, then such training may not only improve sustained attention, but should also improve orientation to the left side of space (given the close connections between the sustained attention and the spatial orientation systems).

A recent study by Robertson et al. (1995) employed this approach with a number of patients suffering from long standing unilateral neglect. Most patients with severe unilateral neglect also show problems with sustained attention. The procedures involved training subjects to improve their internal, or endogenous, control of attention by "talking themselves through it" in a fixed series of stages. The aim of this treatment was to bring attention to the task under voluntary verbal control, and thereby reduce distractibility and improve the length of concentration.

In the sustained attention training procedure, patients were trained while doing a variety of tasks that did not emphasise lateralised scanning: periodically the patients had their attention drawn to the task by combining a loud noise with an instruction to attend. The patient was then gradually taught to "take over" this alerting procedure, so that eventually it became a self-alerting procedure, along the lines described in the Box 6.1.

The results of this training with eight patients were very encouraging. Not only were there improvements in sustained attention, but there were also improvements on spatial neglect over and above those expected by naturally recovery. Figure 6.7 shows the results for the group during the baseline period, during the training period, and at least 24 hours after the last training session. (Incidentally, one patient's cooking improved after training: before training the cheese on the pizza he made was skewed over to the right, while after training he made it with the cheese evenly distributed over the pizza!)

One possibility why this treatment was successful in the short term is that many patients show greater awareness for problems with sustained attention than they do for similar problems with unilateral neglect. If this is true, then such patients may be more likely to implement the training procedure and to employ it in everyday life. It should be noted, however, that as yet there are no data on the longer term effects of this training, as is the case for several of the new treatment methods described in this chapter.

TRAINING TO IMPROVE AWARENESS IN UNILATERAL NEGLECT

Given the fact that most patients with neglect are typically unaware of the functional implications of their condition, it is hardly surprising that it remains a major predictor of poor outcome following stroke (Gialanella & Mattioli,

BOX 6.1   Sustained attention training method (Robertson, et al., 1995)

Training was done in the context of a number of tasks requiring vigilance, including sorting coins, cards, and figures of different colours, sizes, and shapes. These tasks were quite different from the tests used in the evaluation and are described below: the purpose of these tasks was to provide a medium within which the self-alerting or sustained attention training could be taught. The stages of training are outlined below.

1. The person carried one out of these tasks, and errors were pointed out to him/her.
2. The nature of sustained attention/alertness problems were then explained to the person, and the rationale for the training strategy also explained. This rationale was presented in colloquial terms, namely, that it is possible to use undamaged parts of the brain (i.e. the language system) to modulate and activate the impaired parts of the brain, namely, the sustained attention centres of the right hemisphere.
3. The person was required to carry out the task again, and the trainer knocked loudly and unpredictably on the desk on average every 20–40 seconds and said "Attend!" in a loud voice.
4. After several repetitions of step 3, the person said "Attend!" when the trainer knocked on the desk, and the trainer said nothing.
5. After several repetitions of the above, the person was cued to rap the desk at roughly the same frequency as the trainer had. The person said out loud "Attend!" at the same time.
6. The person now rapped the desk and said "Attend!" subvocally.
7. The person now simply signalled whenever he/she was "mentally" knocking the desk and telling him/herself to "pay attention". If this was not done, he/she was cued by the trainer to implement the strategy.
8. Finally, subjects were told about the desirability of trying to apply this strategy habitually in everyday life situations, whereby they could monitor their attention to any particular task.

1992). Can neglect be reduced by trying to improve awareness of the deficits that result from it?

A study in Sweden investigated this question (Söderback, Bengtsson, Ginsburg, & Ekholm, 1992). Patients were videotaped while engaging in routine household tasks that they considered important and relevant to their lives. They were then shown the videotape recording, and the video stopped where the neglect behaviour was most significant. Patients were then led to perceive and interpret the recorded behaviour as indicative of the effects of neglect and given strategies for the relearning and remediation of the condition. This preliminary program requires further evaluation before it can be recommended as an adjunctive form of remediation for neglect.

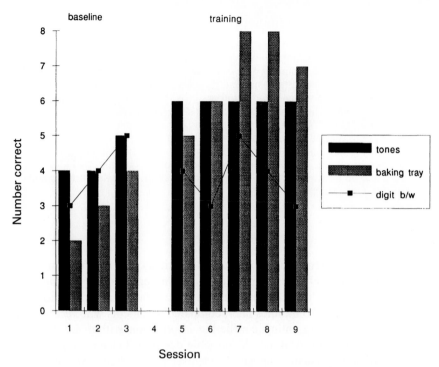

FIG. 6.7   Improvements in unilateral neglect and in ability to sustain attention as a result of sustained attention training.

Oliver Sacks (1983) describes one fascinating case where providing feedback on the consequence of neglect was far from helpful. Sacks points out that knowing something conceptually and knowing it inferentially are two quite separate states of mind. Sack's case is briefly described in Box 6.2.

Another way to improve a patient's awareness involves placing different sense modalities in direct conflict. In one study (Robertson, Nico, & Hood, 1997) patients were required to point to the centre of long metal rods. As with other bisection tasks, patients with unilateral left-sided neglect tended to indicate the centre as located too far to the right of centre. Patients were then given a small number of trials where they picked up the metal rods on the basis of their visual estimate, and so experienced the conflict between their visual estimate (where they had pointed) and the proprioceptive feedback (the sense of unbalance when they attempted to pick up at this point).

As they picked up these long metal rods with their thumb and forefinger, patients were permitted to change their grasp, demonstrating that they were

BOX 6.2   Mirroring neglect

Mrs S., an intelligent lady in her sixties, suffered a severe stroke which gave rise to neglect. She often complained that food was missing from her plate. After applying make-up she found it distressing when she found that she had only made up half of her face. She maintained that when she looked in the mirror she could "see" all. Sacks wondered whether since she could not look left it was possible "for her to have a 'mirror' such that she would see the left side of her face on the right". That is, as someone facing her would see her. They tried a video system, with a camera and monitor facing her. The results, however, were bizarre. Although she did see the left side of her face to her right using the video screen as a "mirror", because the left side of her face and body had no feeling and no existence for her, the effect on Mrs S. was one of distress and bewilderment. (Sacks, 1983, p. 74)

indeed aware that their grip was not central. Patients who received this *brief* feedback (just nine chances to pick up a rod in approximately 2 minutes) showed significantly reduced omissions on cancellation and deviations on bisection tasks up to 30 minutes later, compared to patients who received no such feedback. By presenting conflicting information within the patients' intact sensory modalities, it may be possible that proprioceptive and kinaesthetic information persuades them of the incorrectness of their visual bisection. This approach has to be clinically evaluated, and the short-term improvements in neglect observed may not generalise over a longer period. The principle of utilising other sensory feedback may, however, be worthy of further consideration with a view to developing more clinically effective treatments.

CALORIC STIMULATION

One of the most striking procedures that dramatically improves visual neglect is caloric stimulation. Caloric stimulation is a well-known diagnostic test for measuring the integrity of the vestibular ocular reflex. The vestibular system is concerned with the spatial orientation of the body and information derived from receptors within the vestibular system is used together with visual and proprioceptive inputs to control and modulate body posture. If visual neglect can in part be attributed to a cerebral-induced bias of gaze and postural turning, then it may be possible using a brainstem-mediated vestibular reflex to produce eye movement deviation in a direction opposite the pathologically acquired bias and so reduce the behavioural effects.

Technically, caloric stimulation involves syringing ice-cold water into the ear in order to demonstrate dysfunction in the vestibular system. For the purposes of remediating neglect, the caloric test consists of syringing cold water into the patient's left ear while they lie on a couch with their head raised 30° above the horizontal. When iced water is placed in the patient's left ear, there is often a dramatic improvement in unilateral neglect, however, this is only temporary and often lasts only 15–20 minutes. In addition to the subjective sensation of spatial displacement, the procedure produces a slow wave nystagmus which causes the patient to move his eyes towards the left side. Studies of caloric stimulation have shown short-lasting facilitation of eye- and head-turning toward the neglected left side.

In 1985, Rubens studied the performances of 18 stroke patients with left-sided visual neglect on various tests of visual neglect before and 5 minutes after caloric stimulation. Except for one patient, all stroke patients improved on a battery of tests including line crossing, word reading, and visual scanning. Although the strength of the effect was striking, improvements were, however, transitory, and most of the symptoms returned within several minutes. Over the years the range of neglect-related deficits positively affected by caloric stimulation has increased to include personal neglect, anosognosia and somatoparaphrenia (Cappa et al., 1987; Bisiach, Rusconi, & Vallar 1991). In addition, Rode and Perenin (1994) have shown that vestibular stimulation could also be used to reduce representational or imaginal forms of neglect. In their study, representational neglect was shown in eight patients who were asked to name as many towns as possible from each side of a vertical line splitting an imaginary map of France in half. Baseline performances were much poorer on the left than on the right. After caloric irrigation, left-side scores improved for all patients while right scores remained unchanged.

Another study by Vallar et al. (1990) suggested that the procedure might also be a useful diagnostic technique in distinguishing primary sensory loss from severe sensory inattention. These authors found evidence of normal but temporary, remission of left sensory loss in three right brain damaged patients with severe neglect after using vestibular stimulation. These authors concluded that the attentional factors observed in neglect may in fact be playing a role in the formal testing of what are thought of as "primary" sensory deficit.

Caloric stimulation may facilitate the training of patients with neglect to attend to stimuli in the neglected field. Habituation develops rapidly and may result in long-lasting diminished responsiveness to repeated stimulation. A longitudinal case study by Marshall and Maynard (1983), however, demonstrated that weekly administrations of caloric stimulation enabled a right brain damaged patient to regain full voluntary extraocular eye movements.

It still remains to be shown whether caloric stimulation may be usefully applied in training patients with hemispatial neglect in the clinical rehabilitation setting. At present, it is not certain how vestibular stimulation brings about this temporary remission of neglect. Brain blood flow studies have shown widespread activation of an underactivated right hemisphere during caloric stimulation (Bottini et al., 1994). Rubens (1985) suggested that the vestibular response countered the effect of hemihypokinesia on tests of neglect. Precise theoretical explanations of how vestibular stimulation may work have been proposed, but no clear consensus exists.

VIBROTACTILE STIMULATION
OF THE NECK MUSCLES

When normals and subjects with left-sided neglect are asked to direct a laser pointer to a position exactly 'straight ahead' of their body, normal subjects generally choose orientations close to the objective body midline position, whereas patients with neglect tend to produce subjective body orientations that are typically located more than 15° to the right of the objective orientation.

Karnath, Christ, and Hartje (1993) described the effects of neck muscle vibration and spatial orientation of trunk midline in three patients who showed marked left sided neglect when their trunk, head, and gaze oriented straight ahead. This study found that neglect could be reduced by vibrating the left posterior neck muscles as well as by turning the trunk 15° to the left. Non-specific stimulation on the patient's left side (produced by vibrating the left-hand muscles) had no beneficial effects. The results of this study were interpreted as showing that incoming proprioceptive information from the left posterior neck muscles (produced by turning the trunk or by vibrating the neck muscles) produced remission in the patients' contralateral neglect by producing a shift in the subjective position of the sagittal midplane, which in the case of neglect patients is abnormally oriented to the right.

Karnath (1994) also showed that neglect patients' horizontal displacement of the sagittal midplane to the right could be compensated by neck muscle vibration. These results supported Karnath's hypothesis that one of the essential features of neglect is a disturbance of cortical structures involved in transforming sensory input coordinates from the peripheral sensory organs (e.g. the retina and neck muscle spindles) into egocentric, body centred coordinate frames of reference. In many neglect patients, the systematic error and deviation of the spatial reference frame to the ipsilesional side leads to a corresponding displacement of subjective localisation of body orientation.

Vallar et al. (1995) described the effects of using transcutaneous electrical nerve stimulation (TENS) on patients with left visuospatial hemineglect. Left stimulation applied to the left neck of a group of patients with right hemisphere lesions temporarily improved neglect in 13 out of 14 patients; stimulation of the right neck had no positive effects and indeed produced worse performance in 9 patients. Using TENS, stimulation of both the left hand and left neck had comparable positive effects on visuospatial hemineglect. A further study by Vallar, Rusconi, and Barnardini (1996) with 10 right brain damaged patients again showed that transcutaneous electrical stimulation improved somato-sensory processing transiently after stimulation of the side of the neck contralateral to the side of lesion. Vallar and his colleagues interpreted their results as similar to those of vestibular stimulation. The TENS and vestibular stimulation support both a non-specific activation of the right hemisphere (contralateral to the stimulation side) and a more specific directional effect of left somatosensory stimulation on the egocentric coordinates of extrapersonal space, as suggested by Karnath, Christ, and Hartje (1993). The suggestion is that these interventions by modulating afferent sensory pathways stimulate higher-order spatial representations of the body that have been pathologically distorted.

MONOCULAR EYE PATCHING

After surgical lesions of the posterior cortex, animal studies report disturbances in visual perception and visually guided behaviour resembling that of spatial neglect. Remarkably, these behaviours often improve when a second lesion is made to the contralesional superior colliculus, a small structure located in the subcortical part of the brain that is thought to be responsible for orienting eye movements (Sprague, 1966). Each colliculus receives more ipsilateral than contralateral input from the eyes. The explanation for this effect suggests that recovery of spatial functioning is achieved by dis-inhibiting the effects of the intact ipsilesional superior colliculus. Since retinal input to the superior colliculus is predominantly contralateral, Posner et al., (1987) proposed the idea of producing "functional" lesions similar to those in animals by simply patching ipsilateral visual input.

By patching the ipsilesional (right) eye in patients with neglect, they hypoth-esised that it might be possible to reduce neglect because it reduces the ipsilateral collicular activation by inhibiting the healthy collicular neurons that produced left inattention. On the other hand, left eye patching might make things worse for the patient. To investigate the efficacy of the procedure as a rehabilitation strategy, several researchers have employed monocular eye patching. The results to date remain far from conclusive.

In 1992, Butter and Kirsch reported that 11 out of 13 stroke patients with left-sided neglect benefited from monocular patching on at least one of five different tests of visual neglect. The beneficial effect, however ,was restricted to the period when the patch was worn. Serfaty et al. (1995) tested a group of 26 right hemisphere damaged patients with neglect under binocular and monoc-ular (left and right) viewing conditions. Thirteen of these patients showed improvement of left neglect under left monocular viewing, as compared with the binocular state, 11 patients showed no significant change in either right or left viewing conditions, and 2 patients benefited from right monocular viewing.

Although the result resembles the Sprague effect, these authors suggested that even where the Sprague effect takes place, it would still only appear to be one of several important contributing factors involved in reducing neglect. Recently, Walker, Young, and Lincoln (1996) evaluated the effects of eye patching on 9 patients with left neglect and found that it did not produce a consistent reduction in the severity of neglect. These authors concluded that eye patching was unlikely to be of general use in the rehabilitation of neglect.

LATERALISED KINETIC VISUAL CUEING

Many treatments of neglect involve the use of verbal and non-verbal cues to encourage patients to orient to the neglected side. Most visual cues employed are, however, static, e.g. a coloured line located on the left side of a page. However, given that normal spatial attention is controlled by several different neural systems (Posner & Peterson, 1990) more dynamic stimuli may provide a more salient cue.

To evaluate the effectiveness of dynamic over static cueing, Butter, Kirsch, and Reeves (1990) studied 18 patients with unilateral (left-sided) spatial neglect following right hemisphere stroke. Dynamic visual stimuli (i.e. a flickering light) presented to the left side substantially reduced neglect on a line bisection task. Static stimuli reduced neglect significantly less, whereas dynamic stimuli presented to the centre had no effect on neglect. Neglect patients with hemianopia did not show significantly less benefit for left-sided dynamic stimuli compared to neglect patients without hemianopia, suggesting that the effect of these stimuli may have been largely automatic.

A further study by Butter (1992), in another group of stroke patients ($n = 18$) with left-sided neglect, demonstrated substantial improvements using both monocular patching and/or lateralised visual stimulation. The two procedures combined resulted in significantly larger benefits than either alone. The findings suggest that monocular patching, when used together with lateralised visual stimulation, may further reduce neglect in some daily activities. Recently, Butter and Kirsch (1995) described a further use of dynamic cueing on a visual search task using a laptop computer. Patients with left neglect ($n = 11$) searched for a single target letter among distracter letters presented on a display screen while kinetic visual cues were continuously presented on the left side or the centre of the display screen. Although this left side cueing improved patients' detection of left-sided targets, it did not reduce the time required to search for left-sided targets. Target cues presented in the centre of the display screen did not alter the patients' detection or rate of search for left-sided targets. The authors suggest that kinetic visual cues may be more suitable than other forms of cueing for rehabilitation of neglect and may be particularly effective with neglect patients whose attention is strongly biased to the right.

OPTOKINETIC STIMULATION

As we saw earlier, neglect performance may be improved after caloric stimulation. It is possible that the slow wave eye movement (nystagmus) produced towards the left in this condition may facilitate changes in the attentional system, enabling the patient to attend more to left-sided space. Another method that produces a similar nystagmus is that of "optokinetic stimulation". This reflex is normally produced by requiring a subject to look at a slow-moving shape. A recent study by Pizzamiglio, Frasca, Guariglia, Incoccia, and Antonucci (1990) examined the effects of optokinetic stimulation on three groups of subjects, controls, and right brain damaged patients, with and without neglect. Subjects were required to bisect lines in the presence of a fixed or a moving optokinetic inducing background. When the stimulus was moved horizontally towards the left or the right, it produced an optokinetic nystagmus and lead to a displacement of the subjective midpoint when compared with a fixed background, in all three groups. Within the neglect patient group, this displacement on line bisection was greatest for stimuli moving toward the right. The effect of the optokinetic stimulation was present in most cases and proved to be relatively stable in a test/retest presentation. Given the relatively simple situation and the reduced unpleasantness when compared with caloric stimulation it is possible that optokinetic stimulation could provide a relatively benign adjunct to treatments of neglect.

MEDICATION

Neglect in animals with frontal lesions have been shown to improve with apomorphine, a dopamine agonist (Corwin et al., 1986). Attempts to remediate neglect using medication are, however, still rare. One of the few clinical trials of a dopamine agonist therapy was carried out by Fleet, Valenstein, Watson, and Heilman (1987) in the case of two patients with contralesional hemispatial neglect. Using 15mg of bromocriptine (a dopamine agonist) daily for 3 to 4 weeks, both patients were evaluated on several neglect tests before, during, and after treatment. Tests were repeated on different days in each phase to decrease spontaneous variability. Bromocriptine was chosen because it could be orally administered and was commonly used in such "low-dose" forms in parkinsonian patients and patients with pituitary tumours. Neglect significantly improved with medication and worsened after its withdrawal in both patients. Neither patient showed any side effects. Recovery was, however, incomplete. Both patients continued to make errors associated with neglect on individual subtests, although now significantly diminished. The authors conclude that despite the open nature of this trial (only two cases), the positive results warrant larger controlled studies.

THE USE OF PRISMS TO IMPROVE NEGLECT

Although neglect is regarded by most psychologists and neurologists as a disorder of selective attention affecting the left spatial field, it is not altogether surprising to discover attempts to reduce the functional consequences of visual neglect or hemianopia by use of wide-angled lens (Drasdo, 1976), closed circuit TV monitoring systems (Turner, 1976), and mirrors attached to the special frame (Nerenberg, 1980).

More recently, Rossi, Kheyfets, and Reding (1990) described a randomised study evaluating the effectiveness of 15-diopter plastic press-on heminaopic Fresnel lens attached to the patient's glasses. An example of the experimental set-up using the glasses is shown in Fig. 6.8. This study randomly assigned patients with stroke and homonymous hemianopia or unilateral visual neglect (extinction) to the "treatment" with the Fresnel prisms or control lenses. Baseline evaluations on visual perception, neglect, and activities of daily living (ADL) were similar for both groups. After 4 weeks, the prism-treated group performed significantly better than controls on several tests sensitive to

FIG. 6.8   Illustrating use of Fresnel prisms. Example of a patient with right hemianopia with prisms applied over the right hemifield with base of prisms directed towards patient's right. Reprinted with permission of Lippincott, Williams, and Wilkins from Rossi, P.W., Kheyfets, S., and Reding, M.J. (1990). Fresnel prisms improve visual perception in stroke patients with homonymous hemianopia or unilateral visual neglect. *Neurology, 40*, 1597–1599.

neglect, though there was no significant difference on the Barthel ADL assessment at 4 weeks. The authors concluded that although treatment with Fresnel prisms appeared to improve visual perception test scores, no improvement on functional tasks was observed. Unfortunately, this study did not distinguish between patients with visual field deficits and those with visual neglect. Furthermore, the use of the term "visual neglect" was inappropriate as one of the screening tests used evaluated extinction—the inability to reliably detect bilateral tachistoscopically presented targets—rather than what is conventionally understood as visual neglect.

More recently, striking improvements in neglect for 2 hours after prism use have been observed. In this study (Rossetti, Rode, Pisela, Farné, Li, Boisson, & Perenin, 1998), patients learned to make motor responses to objects in the distorted field. This perceptual motor training may have been important in producing the observed changes.

CONCLUSIONS

The development of practical rehabilitation methods for neglect remains in its infancy. As yet there is no conclusive evidence from randomised controlled trials that any one particular treatment is overwhelmingly effective, though a number of single-case studies have generated promising results.

Training patients to scan to the left appears both intuitive and straightforward and there are some reports where in some patients it has been useful, particularly if the scanning training involves real-life contexts where the patients are more likely to remember to engage in compensatory scanning. Patients can be taught to use their left arm as an "anchor" or cue to remember to attend to the left side. Encouraging those patients who can move their hands to make small movements with the left side of their body may also reduce neglect in some cases.

Neglect is also affected by processes which have no immediately obvious connection to the bias of attention towards the right. For instance, improving sustained attention can produce specific improvements in left neglect, and widening the attentional spotlight by right-sided cueing has also exciting possibilities, although the latter has not yet been clinically evaluated. This is also the case for a number of other promising interventions that have only produced short-term reductions in neglect and which are described in this chapter.

The work by Taub and colleagues (1993), which shows that, in a proportion of non-neglecting hemiplegic patients, discouraging the use of the unaffected limb can result in improved function in the affected limb, is also of potential relevance to neglect. As we have shown, neglect may be a problem caused not just by under activation of the damaged right hemisphere, but may also be exacerbated by over activation of the non-damaged left hemisphere.

Unilateral spatial neglect is clearly not a unitary phenomenon, and treatment almost certainly will have to be tailored to the particular characteristics of the problem in any particular patient. In this book we have tried to give practical guidelines about the assessment of neglect, with an eye to the underlying neuropsychological problems—which are sometimes complex.

We have also shown that there are certain types of treatment that appear to improve function following unilateral spatial neglect. We have also reviewed a number of other promising treatment procedures that are not yet clinically validated, but we can expect to see major improvements in the therapeutic possibilities for this troubling disorder in the future.

What also emerges from this book is the possibility that some types of motor and sensory deficits following right hemisphere stroke may actually be exacerbated, or even in some cases mainly caused, by spatial attempts at attentional deficits related to neglect of the left side of the body. It may well be that some treatments for unilateral neglect may end up having effects far more widespread than simply on the biased attentional system within the visual modality.

In general, however, it is up to therapists and clinicians to throw up challenges for researchers in this area, so that a proper blending of theory and practice can take place to the ultimate benefit of patients.

References

Albert, M. (1973). A simple test of visual neglect. *Neurology, 23*, 658–664.

Anton, H.A., Hershler, H.C., Lloyd, P., & Murray, D. (1988). Visual neglect and extinction: A new test. *Archives of Physical Medicine and Rehabilitation, 69*, 1013–1016.

Antonucci, G., Guariglia, C., Judica, A., Magnotti, L., Paolucci, S., Pizzamiglio, L., & Zoccolotti, P. (1995). Effectiveness of neglect rehabilitation in a randomized group study. *Journal of Clinical and Experimental Neuropsychology, 17*, 383–389.

Azouvi, P., Marchal, F., Samuel, C., Morin, L., Renard, C., Louis-Dreyfus, A., Jokic, C., Wiart, L., Pradat-Diehl, P., Deloche, G., & Bergego, C. (1996). Functional consequences and awareness of unilateral neglect: Study of an evaluation scale. *Neuropsychological Rehabilitation, 6*, 133–150.

Babinski, J. (1914). Contribution a l'etude des troubles mentaux dans l'hemiplegie organique cerebrale (Anosognosie). *Revue Neurologique, 27*, 845–848.

Barbut, D., & Gazzaniga, M. (1987). Disturbances in conceptual space involving language and speech. *Brain, 110*, 1487–1496.

Battersby, W.S., Bender, M.B., Pollack, M., Kahn, R.L. (1956). Unilateral 'spatial agnosia' ("inattention") in patients with cerebral lesions. *Brain, 79*, 68–93.

Beis, J.-M., André, J.-M., & Saguez, A. (1994). Detection of visual field deficits and visual neglect with computerized light emitting diodes. *Archives of Physical Medicine and Rehabilitation, 75*, 711–714.

Berti, A., & Rizzalotti, G. (1992). Visual processing without awareness: Evidence from unilateral neglect. *Journal of Cognitive Neuroscience, 4*, 345–351.

Beschin, N., Cocchini, G., Della Sala, S., & Logie, R.H. (1997). What the eyes perceive, the brain ignores: A case of pure unilateral representational neglect. *Cortex, 33*, 3–16.

Beschin, N., & Robertson, I.H. (1997). Personal and extrapersonal neglect following stroke. *Cortex, 33*, 379–384.

Bisiach, E., & Geminiani, G. (1991). Anosognosia related to hemiplegia and hemianopia. In G. Prigatano and D.L. Schacter (Eds.) *Awareness of deficit after brain injury.* New York: Academic Press.

Bisiach, E., Geminiani, G., Berti, A., & Rusconi, M. (1990). Perceptual and premotor factors of unilateral neglect. *Neurology, 40*, 1278–1281.

Bisiach, E., & Luzzatti, C. (1978). Unilateral neglect of representational space. *Cortex, 14*, 129–133.

Bisiach, E., Perani, D., Vallar, G., & Berti, A. (1986). Unilateral neglect: Personal and extra-personal. *Neuropsychologia, 24*, 759–767.

Bisiach, E., & Rusconi, M.L. (1990). Breakdown of perceptual awareness in unilateral neglect. *Cortex, 26*, 1–7.

Bisiach, E., Rusconi, M.L., & Vallar, G. (1991). Remission of somatoparaphrenic delusion through vestibular stimulation. *Neuropsychologia, 29*, 1029–1031.

Bottini, G., Sterzi, R., Paulesu, E., Vallar, G., Cappa, S.F., Erminio, F., Passingham, R.E., Frith, C.D., & Frackowiak, R.S.J. (1994). Identification of central vestibular projections in man: A positron emission tomography activation study. *Experimental Brain Research, 99*, 164–169.

Bradshaw, J.L., & Mattingley, J.B. (1966). *Clinical neuropsychology: Behaviour and brain science*. New York: Academic Press.

Brouchon, M., Joanette, Y., & Sampson, M. (1985). From movement to gesture: "Here" and "there" as determinants of visually guided pointing. In J.L. Nespoulous and A.R. Lecours (Eds.). *Biological foundations of gestures: Motors and semiotic aspects*. Hillsdale, NJ: Erlbaum.

Butter, C.M. (1992). Effect of stimuli in right hemipsace on left-sided neglect in a line cancellation task. *Neurospsychologia, 30*, 859–864.

Butter, C.M., & Kisch, N. (1992). Combined and separate effects of eye patching and visual stimulation on unilateral neglect following stroke. *Archives of Physical Medicine and Rehabilitation, 73*, 1133–1139.

Butter, C.M., Kirsch, N., & Reeves, G. (1990). The effect of lateralized dynamic stimuli on unilateral spatial neglect following right hemisphere lesions. *Restorative Neurology and Neuroscience, 2*, 39–46.

Butter, C.M., & Kirsch, N. (1995). Effect of lateralized kinetic visual cues on visual search in patients with unilateral spatial neglect. *Journal of Clinical and Experimental Neuropsychology, 17*, 856–867.

Calvanio, R., Levine, D.N., & Petrone, D. (1993). Elements of cognitive rehabilitation after right hemisphere stroke. *Behavioural Neurology, 11*, 25–57.

Campbell, D.C., & Oxbury, J.M. (1976). Recovery from unilateral visuospatial neglect. *Cortex, 12*, 303–312.

Caplan, B. (1987). Assessment of unilateral neglect: A new reading test. *Journal of Clinical and Experimental Neuropsychology, 9*, 359–364.

Cappa, S., Sterzi, R., Vallar, G., & Bisiach, E. (1987). Remission of hemineglect and anosognosia during vestibular stimulation. *Neuropsychologia, 25*, 775–782.

Chamorro, A., Sacco, R.L., Ciecierski, K., Binder, J.R., Tatemichi, T.K., & Mohr, J.P. (1990). Visual hemineglect and hemihallucinations in a patient with subcortical infarction. *Neurology, 40*, 1463–1464.

Chen Sea, M.J., Henderson, A., & Cermak, S.A. (1993). Patterns of visual spatial inattention and their functional significance in stroke patients. *Archives of Physical Medicine and Rehabilitation, 74*, 355–360.

Cherington, M. (1974). Visual neglect in a chess player. *Journal of Nervous and Mental Disease, 159*, 145–147.

Corwin, J.V., Kanter, S., Watson, R.T., Heilman, K.M., Valenstein, E., & Hashimoto, A. (1986). Apomorphine has a therapeutic effect on neglect produced by unilateral dorsomedial prefrontal cortex lesions in rats. *Experimental Neurology, 36*, 683–698.

Coslett, H.B., Bowers, D., Fitzpatrick, E., Haws, B., & Heilman, K.M. (1990). Directional hypokinesia and hemispatial inattention in neglect. *Brain, 113*, 475–486.

Cubelli, R., Pugliese, M., & Gabellini, A.S. (1994). The effect of space location on neglect depends on the nature of the task. *Journal of Neurology, 241,* 611–614.

Cutting, J. (1978). Study of anosognosia. *Journal of Neurology, Neurosurgery and Psychiatry, 41,* 548–555.

Denes, G., Semenza, C., Stoppa, E., & Lis, A. (1982). Unilateral spatial neglect and recovery from hemiplegia. *Brain, 105,* 543–552.

Diller, L., & Weinberg, J. (1997). Hemi-inattention in rehabilitation: The evolution of a rational remediation program. In E. Weinstein & R. Friedland (Eds.), *Advances in Neurology* (pp. 63–82). New York: Raven Press.

Doricchi, F., Guariglia, C., Paolucci, S., & Pizzamiglio, L. (1991). Disappearance of leftward rapid eye movements during sleep in left visual hemi-inattention. *NeuroReport, 2,* 285–288.

Drasdo, N. (1976). Visual field expanders. *American Journal of Optometry and Physiological Optics, 53,* 464–467.

Driver, J., & Halligan, P.W. (1991). Can visual neglect operate in object-centred coordinates? An affirmative single case study. *Cognitive Neuropsychology, 8,* 475–496.

Edgeworth, J., Robertson, I.H., & MacMillan, T. (1998). *The Balloons Test.* Bury St Edmunds: Thames Valley Test Company.

Fanthome, Y., Lincoln, N.B., Drummond, A., & Walker, M.F. (1995). The treatment of visual neglect using feedback of eye movements: A pilot study. *Disability and Rehabilitation, 17,* 413–417.

Fleet, W.S., & Heilman, K.M. (1986). The fatigue effect in unilateral neglect. *Neurology, 36,* 258.

Fleet, W.S., Valenstien, E., Watson, R.T., & Heilman, K.M. (1987). Dopamine agonist therapy for neglect in humans. *Neurology, 37,* 1765–1771.

Friedman, P.J. (1992). The star cancellation test in acute stroke. *Clinical Rehabilitation, 6,* 23–30.

Fullerton, K.J., Mackenzie, G., & Stout, R.W. (1988). Prognostic indices in stroke. *Quarterly Journal of Medicine, 66(250),* 147–162.

Gainotti, G., D'Erme, P., & Bartolomeo, P. (1991). Early orientation of attention toward the half space ipsilateral to the lesion in patients with unilateral brain damage. *Journal of Neurology, Neurosurgery and Psychiatry, 54,* 1082–1089.

Gainotti, G., Monteleone, D., & Silveri, M.C. (1986). Mechanisms of unilateral spatial neglect in relation to laterality of cerebral lesions. *Brain, 88,* 337–294, 585–644.

Gardner, H. (1982). *Art, mind and brain: A cognitive approach to creativity.* New York: Basic Books.

Gassell, M.M., & Williams, D. (1963). Visual function in patients with homonymous hemianopia. The completion phenomenon: Insight and attitude to the defect and visual function efficiency. *Brain, 86,* 229–260.

Gauthier, L., Dehaut, F., & Joanette, Y. (1989). The Bells Test: A quantitative and qualitative test for visual neglect. *International Journal of Clinical Neuropsychology, 11,* 49–54.

Gialanella, B., & Mattioli, F. (1992). Anosognosia and extrapersonal neglect as predictors of functional recovery following right hemisphere stroke. *Neuropsychological Rehabilitation, 2,* 169–178.

Goodale, M.A., Milner, A.D., Jakobson, L.S., & Carey, S.P. (1990). Kinematic analysis of limb movements in neuropsychological research: Subtle deficits and recovery of function. *Canadian Journal of Psychology, 44,* 180–195.

Grossi, D., Angelini, R., Pecchinenda, A., & Pizzamiglio, L. (1993). Left imaginal neglect in hemi-inattention: Experimental study with the o'clock test. *Behavioural Neurology, 6,* 155–158.

Guariglia, C., & Antonucci, G. (1992) Personal and extrapersonal space: A case of neglect dissociation. *Neuropsychologia, 30,* 1001–1009.

Guariglia, C., Padovani, A., Pantano, P., & Pizzamiglio, L. (1993). Unilateral neglect restricted to visual imagery. *Nature, 364,* 235–237.

Halligan, P.W. (1995). Drawing attention to neglect: The contribution of line bisection. The *Psychologist, 8,* 257–264.

Halligan, P.W., & Cockburn, J. (1993). Cognitive sequelae of stroke: Visuospatial and memory disorders. *Critical Reviews in Physical and Rehabilitation Medicine, 5,* 57–81.

Halligan, P.W., Cockburn, J., & Wilson, B. (1991a). The behavioural assessment of visual neglect. *Neuropsychological Rehabilitation, 1,* 5–32.

Halligan, P.W., Donegan, C., & Marshall, J.C. (1992). When is a cue not a cue? On the intractability of visuospatial neglect. *Neuropsychological Rehabilitation, 2,* 283–293.

Halligan, P.W., Manning, L., & Marshall, J.C. (1990a). Hemispheric activation vs spatio-motor cueing in visual neglect: A case study. *Nia, 29,* 165–176.

Halligan, P.W., & Marshall, J.C. (1988). How long is a piece of string? A study of line bisection in a case of visual neglect. *Cortex, 24,* 321–328.

Halligan, P.W., & Marshall, J.C. (1989a). Laterality of motor response in visuospatial neglect: A case study. *Neuropsychologia, 27,* 1301–1307.

Halligan, P.W., & Marshall, J.C. (1989b). Line bisection in visuospatial neglect: Disproof of a conjecture. *Cortex, 25,* 517–521.

Halligan, P.W., & Marshall, J.C. (1989c). Perceptual cueing and perceptuo-motor compatibility in visuospatial neglect: A single case study. *Cognitive Neurospychology, 6,* 423–435.

Halligan, P.W., & Marshall, J.C. (1989d). Two techniques for the assessment of line bisection in visuospatial neglect: A single case study. *Journal of Neurology, Neurosurgery and Psychiatry, 52,* 1300–1302.

Halligan, P.W., & Marshall, J.C. (1991a). Figural modulation of visuospatial neglect: A case study. *Neuropsychologia, 29,* 619–628.

Halligan, P.W., & Marshall, J.C. (1991b). Left neglect for near but not far space in man. *Nature, 350,* 498–500.

Halligan, P.W., & Marshall, J.C. (1992). Left visuospatial neglect: A meaningless entity? *Cortex, 28,* 525–535.

Halligan, P.W., & Marshall, J.C. (1993a). Homing in on neglect: A case study of visual search. *Cortex, 29,* 167–174.

Halligan, P.W., & Marshall, J.C. (1993b). When two is one: A case study of spatial parsing in visual neglect. *Perception, 22,* 309–312.

Halligan, P.W., & Marshall, J.C. (1994a). Completion in visuospatial neglect: A case study. *Cortex, 30,* 685–694.

Halligan, P.W., & Marshall, J.C. (1994b). Focal and global attention modulate the expression of visual-spatial neglect: A case study. *Neuropsychologia, 32,* 13–21.

Halligan, P.W., & Marshall, J.C. (1994c). Right sided cueing can ameliorate left neglect? *Neuropsychological Rehabilitation, 4,* 63–73.

Halligan, P.W., & Marshall, J.C. (1994d). Towards a principled explanation of unilateral neglect. *Cognitive Neuropsychology, 11,* 167–206.

Halligan, P.W., & Marshall, J.C. (1997). The art of visual neglect. *Lancet, 350,* 139–140.

Halligan, P.W., & Marshall, J.C. (1998). Neglect of awareness. *Consciousness and Cognition, 7,* 356–380.

Halligan, P.W., & Marshall, J.C., & Wade, D.T. (1989). Visuospatial neglect: Underlying factors and test sensitivity. *Lancet,* October 14, 980–910.

Halligan, P.W., & Marshall, J.C., & Wade, D.T. (1990b). Do visual field deficits exacerbate visuospatial neglect? *Journal of Neurology, Neurosurgery and Psychiatry, 53,* 487–491.

Halligan, P.W., & Marshall, J.C., & Wade, D.T. (1993). Three arms: A case study of supernumerary phantom limb after right hemisphere stroke. *Journal of Neurology, Neurosurgery and Psychiatry, 56,* 159–166.

Halligan, P.W., & Marshall, J.C., & Wade, D.T. (1995). Unilateral somatoparaphrenia after right hemisphere stroke: A case description. *Cortex*, *31*, 173–182.

Hartman-Maeir, A., & Katz, N. (1994). Validity of the Behavioural Inattention Test (BIT): Relationships with functional tasks. *The American Journal of Occupational Therapy*, *49*, 507–516.

Heilman, K.M., Watson, R.T., & Valenstein, E. (1993). Neglect and related disorders. In K.M. Heilman & E. Valenstein (Eds.). *Clinical neuropsychology*. New York: Oxford University Press.

Hensen, D.B. (1993). *Visual fields*. Oxford: Oxford Medical Publications.

Herman, E.W.M. (1992). Spatial neglect: New issues and their implications for occupational therapy practice. *The American Journal of Occupational Therapy*, *46*, 207–215.

Hier, D.B., Mondlock, J., & Caplan, L.R. (1983a). Behavioural abnormalities after right hemisphere stroke. *Neurology*, *33*, 337–344.

Hier, D.B., Mondlock, J., & Caplan, L.R. (1983b). Recovery of behavioural abnormalities after right hemisphere stroke. *Neurology*, *33*, 345–350.

House, A., & Hodges, J. (1988). Persistent denial of handicap after infarction of the right basal ganglia: A case study. *Journal of Neurology, Neurosurgery and Psychiatry*, *51*, 112–115.

Ishiai, S., Furukawa, T., & Tsukagoshi, H. (1987). Eye fixation patterns in homonymous hemianopia and unilateral spatial neglect. *Neuropsychologia*, *25*, 675–679.

Jeannerod, M. (Ed.). (1987). *Neurophysiological and neuropsychological aspects of spatial neglect*. North Holland: Elsevier Science Publishers.

Johnson, C.A., & Keltner, J.L. (1983). Incidence of visual field losses in 20,000 eyes and its relationship to driving performance. *Archives of Ophthalmology*, *101*, 371–375.

Kaplan, R.F., Verfaillie, M., Meadows, M., Caplan, L.R., Pessin, M.S., & Dana, DeWitt L. (1991). Changing attentional demands in left hemispatial neglect. *Archives of Neurology*, *48*, 1263–1267.

Karnath, H.O. (1994). Spatial limitation of eye movements during ocular exploration of simple line drawings in neglect syndrome. *Cortex*, *30*, 319–330.

Karnath, H.O., Christ, K., & Hartje, W. (1993). Decrease of contralateral neglect by neck muscle vibration and spatial orientation of trunk midline. *Brain*, *116*, 383–396.

Karnath, H.O., Schenkel, P., & Fischer, B. (1991). Trunk orientation as the determining factor of the 'contralateral' deficit in the neglect syndrome and as the physical anchor of the internal representation of body orientation in space. *Brain*, *114*, 1997–2014.

Kinsbourne, M. (1987). Mechanisms of unilateral neglect. In M. Jeannerod (Ed.), *Neurophysiological and neuropsychological aspects of spatial neglect* (pp. 69–85). North Holland: Elsevier Science Publishers.

Kinsbourne, M. (1993). Orientational bias model of unilateral neglect: Evidence from attentional gradients within hemispace. In I.H. Robertson & J.C. Marshall (Eds.), *Unilateral neglect: Clinical and experimental studies* (pp. 69–85). Hove, UK: Lawrence Erlbaum Associates Ltd.

Kinsella, G., & Ford, B. (1980). Acute recovery patterns in stroke patients. *Medical Journal of Australia*, *2*, 663–666.

Kinsella, G., & Ford, B. (1985). Hemi-inattention and the recovery patterns of stroke patients. *International Rehabilitation Medicine*, *7*, 102–106.

Kolb, B., & Wishaw, I.Q. (1993). *Fundamentals of human neuropsychology* (Third Edition). WH Freeman and Company: New York.

Kooistra, C.A., & Heilman, K.M. (1989). Hemispatial neglect masquerading as hemianopia. *Neurology*, *39*, 1125–1127.

Lachenmayr, B.J., & Vivell, P.M.O. (1993). *Perimetry and its clinical correlations*. Thieme Medical Publishers: New York.

Ladavas, E., Menghini, G. & Umilta, C. (1994). A rehabilitation study of hemispatial neglect. *Cognitive Neuropsychology*, *11*, 75–95.

Lawson, I.R. (1962). Visual-spatial neglect in lesions of the right cerebral hemisphere. *Neurology, 12*, 23–33.

Leicester, J., Sidman, M., Stoddard, L.T., & Mohr, J.F. (1969). Some determinants of visual neglect. *Journal of Neurology, Neuropsychology & Psychiatry, 32*, 580–587.

Lennon, S. (1994). Behavioural rehabilitation in unilateral neglect. In M.J. Riddoch and G.W. Humphreys (Eds.), *Cognitive neuropsychology and cognitive rehabilitation*. Hove, UK: Lawrence Erlbaum Associates Ltd.

Levine, D.N., Calvanio, R., & Rinn, W.E. (1991). The pathogenesis of anosognosia for hemiplegia. *Neurology, 41*, 1770–1781.

Levine, D.N., Warach, J.D., Benowitz, L., & Calvanio, R. (1986). Left spatial neglect: Effects of lesion size and premorbid brain atrophy on severity of recovery following right cerebral infarction. *Neurology, 36*, 362–366.

Levy, D., Blizzard, R.A., Halligan, P.W., & Stone, S.P. (1995). Fluctuations in visual neglect after stroke? *European Neurology, 35*, 341–343.

Lincoln, N.B. (1991). The recognition and treatment of visual perceptual disorders. *Topics in Gereiatric Rehabilitation, 7*, 25–34.

Manly, T., Robertson, I.H., & Verity, C. (1997). Developmental unilateral neglect: A single case study. *Neurocase, 3*, 19–30.

Mark, V.M., Kooistra, C.A., & Heilman, K.M. (1988). Hemispatial neglect affected by non-neglected stimuli. *Neurology, 38*, 1207–1211.

Marshall, C.R., & Maynard, F.M. (1983). Vestibular stimulation for supranuclear gaze palsy: Case report. *Archives of Physical Medicine, 64*, 134–136.

Marshall, J.C., & Halligan, P.W. (1988). Blindsight and insight in visuospatial neglect. *Nature, 336*, 776–777.

Marshall, J.C., & Halligan, P.W. (1989a). Does the mid-saggital plane play any privileged role in "left" neglect? *Cognitive Neuropsychology, 6*, 403–422.

Marshall, J.C., & Halligan, P.W. (1989b). When left goes right: An investigation of line bisection in a case of visual neglect. *Cortex, 25*, 503–515.

Marshall, J.C., & Halligan, P.W. (1991). A study of plane bisection in 4 cases of visual neglect. *Cortex, 27*, 277–284.

Marshall, J.C., & Halligan, P.W. (1993). Visuospatial neglect: A new copying test to assess perceptual parsing. *Journal of Neurology, 240*, 37–40.

Marshall, J.C., & Halligan, P.W. (1995a). Seeing the forest but only half the trees? *Nature, 373*, 521–523.

Marshall, J.C., & Halligan, P.W. (1995b). Within- and between-task dissociations in visuospatial neglect: A case study. *Cortex, 31*, 367–376.

McCarthy, R.A., & Warrington, E.K. (1990). *Cognitive neuropsychology: A clinical introduction*. New York: Academic Press.

McGlinchey-Berroth, R., Milberg, W.P., Verfaillie, M., Alexander, M., & Kilduff, P. (1993). Semantic processing in the neglected visual field: Evidence from a lexical decision task. *Cognitive Neuropsychology, 10*, 79–108.

McIntosh, R.D., Brodie, E.E., Beschin, N., & Robertson, I.H. (in press). Improving the clinical diagnosis of personal neglect: Reforming the Comb and Razor Test. *Cortex.*

Meador, K.J., Loring, D.W., Bowers, D., & Heilman, K.M. (1987). Remote memory and neglect syndrome. *Neurology, 37*, 522–536.

Meichenbaum, D., & Goodman, J. (1971). Training impulsive children to talk to themselves: A means of developing self-control. *Journal of Abnormal Psychology, 77*, 115–126.

Meienberg, O. (1983). Clinical examination of saccadic eye movements in hemianopia. *Neurology, 33*, 1311–1315.

Meienberg, O., Harrer, M., & Wehren, C. (1986). Oculographic diagnosis of hemineglect in patients with homonymous hemianopia. *Journal of Neurology, 233*, 97–101.

Meienberg, O., Zangemeister, W.H., Rosenberg, M., Hoyt, W.F., & Stark, L. (1981). Saccadic eye movement strategies in patients with homonymous hemianopia. *Annals of Neurology, 9,* 537–544.

Mesulam, M. (1981). A cortical network for directed attention and unilateral neglect. *Annals of Neurology, 10,* 309–325.

Milner, A.D., Brechmann, M., & Pagliarini, L. (1992). To halve and to halve not: An analysis if line bisection judgements in normal subjects. *Neuropsychologia, 30,* 515–526.

Nadeau, S.E., & Heilman, K.M. (1991). Gaze-dependent hemianopia without hemispatial neglect. *Neurology, 41,* 1244–1250.

Nerenberg, B. (1980). A new mirror design for hemianopia. *Optics, 57,* 183–186.

Oddy, M., Coughlan, T., Typerman, A. & Jenkins, D. (1985). Social adjustment after closed head injury: a further follow-up seven years after injury. *Journal of Neurology, Neurosurgery and Psychiatry, 48,* 564–568.

Odgen, J.A. (1985). Anterior-posterior interhemispheric differences in the loci of lesions producing visual hemineglect. *Brain and Cognition, 4,* 59–75.

Pardo, J.V., Fox, P.T., & Raichle, M.E. (1991). Localization of a human system for sustained attention by positron emission tomography. *Nature, 349,* 61–64.

Patton, J. (1996). *Neurological differential diagnosis.* Heidelberg: Springer-Verlag.

Pierson-Savage, J.M., Bradshaw, J.L., Bradshaw, J.A., & Nettleton, N.C. (1998). Vibrotactile reaction times in unilateral neglect. *Brain, 111,* 1531–1545.

Pizzamiglio, L., Frasca, R., Guariglia, C., Incoccia, C., & Antonucci, G. (1990). Effect of optokinetic stimulation in patients with visual neglect. *Cortex, 26,* 535–540.

Posner, M.I. (1993). Interaction of arousal and selection in the posterior attention network. In A. Baddeley & L. Weiskrantz (Eds.), *Attention: Selection, awareness and control* (pp. 390–405). Oxford: Clarendon Press.

Posner, M.I., & Peterson, S.E. (1990). The attention system of the human brain. *Annual Review of Neuroscience, 13,* 25–42.

Posner, M.I., Walker, J.A., Friedrich, F.J., & Rafal, R.D. (1984). Effects of parietal injury on covert orienting of attention. *Journal of Neuroscience, 4,* 1863–1874.

Posner, M.I., Walker, J.A., Friedrich, E.F., & Rafal, R.D. (1987). How do the parietal lobes direct cover attention? *Neuropsychologia, 25,* 135–146.

Prigatano, G.P., & Schacter, D.L. (Eds.) (1991). *Awareness of deficit after brain injury.* New York: Oxford University Press.

Rapcsak, S.Z., Verfaellie, M., Fleet, S., & Heilman, K.M. (1989). Selective attention in hemispatial neglect. *Archives of Neurology, 46,* 178–182.

Riddoch, M.J., & Humphreys, G. (1983). The effect of cueing on unilateral neglect. *Neuropsychologia, 21,* 589–599.

Rizzolatti, G., & Gallese, V. (1988). Mechanisms and theories of spatial neglect. In F. Boller and J. Grafman (Eds.), *Handbook of neuropsychology* (Vol 1). Amsterdam: Elsevier.

Robertson, I.H. (1989). Anomalies in the laterality of omissions in unilateral left visual neglect: Implications for an attentional theory of neglect. *Neuropsychologia, 27,* 157–165.

Robertson, I.H., & Cashman, E. (1991). Auditory feedback for walking difficulties in a case of unilateral neglect: A pilot study. *Neuropsychological Rehabilitation, 1,* 175–184.

Robertson, I.H., & Frasca, R. (1992). Attentional load and visual neglect. *International Journal of Neuroscience, 62,* 45–56.

Robertson, I.H., Halligan, P.W., Bergego, C., Hömberg, V., Pizzamiglio, L., Weber, E., & Wilson, B.A. (1994a). Right neglect following right hemisphere damage? *Cortex, 30,* 199–214.

Robertson, I.H., Hogg, K., & McMillan, T.M. (1998). Rehabilitation of unilateral neglect: Reducing inhibitory competition by contralesional limb activation. *Neuropsychological Rehabilitation, 8,* 19–30.

Robertson, I.H., Manly, T., Beschin, N., Daini, R., Haeske-Dewick, H., Hömberg, V., Jehkonen, M., Pizzamiglio, L., Sheil, A., & Weber, E. (1997). Auditory sustained attention is a marker of unilateral spatial neglect. *Neuropsychologia, 35*, 1527–1532.

Robertson, I.H., & Marshall, J.C. (Eds.), (1993). *Unilateral neglect: Clinical and experimental studies*. Hove, UK: Lawrence Erlbaum Associates Ltd.

Robertson, I.H., Mattingley, J.B., Rorden, C., & Driver, J. (1998). Phasic alerting of right hemisphere neglect patients overcomes their spatial deficit awareness. *Nature, 395*, 169–172.

Robertson, I.H., Nico, D., & Hood, B.M. (1997). Believing what you feel: Using proprioceptive feedback to reduce unilateral neglect. *Neuropsychology, 11*, 53–58.

Robertson, I.H., & North, N. (1992). Spatio-motor cueing in unilateral neglect: The role of hemispace, hand and motor activation. *Neuropsychologia, 30*, 553–563.

Robertson, I.H., & North, N. (1994). One hand is better than two: Motor extinction of left hand advantage in unilateral neglect. *Neuropsychologia, 32*, 1–11.

Robertson, I.H., North, N., & Geggie, C. (1992). Spatio-motor cueing in unilateral neglect: Three single case studies of its therapeutic effectiveness. *Journal of Neurology, Neurosurgery and Psychiatry, 55*, 799–805.

Robertson, I.H., Tegnér, R., Tham, K., Lo, A., & Nimmo-Smith, I. (1995). Sustained attention training for unilateral neglect: Theoretical and rehabilitation implications. *Journal of Clinical and Experimental Neuropsychology, 17*, 416–430.

Robertson, I.H., Ward, A., Ridgeway, V., & Nimmo-Smith, I. (1994b). *Test of Everyday Attention*. Flempton: Thames Valley Test Company.

Robertson, I.H., Ward, A., Ridgeway, V., & Nimmo-Smith, I. (1996). The structure of normal human attention: The Test of Everyday Attention. *Journal of International Neuropsychological Society, 2*, 525–534.

Robertson, L.C., (1992). The role of perceptual organisation and search in attentional disorders. In D.I. Margolin (Ed), *Cognitive neuropsychology in clinical practice*. New York: Oxford University Press.

Rode, G., & Perenin, M. (1994). Temporary remission of representation hemineglect through vestibular stimulation. *NeuroReport, 5*, 869–872.

Ross, F.L. (1992). The use of computers in occupational therapy for visual scanning training. *American Journal of Occupational Therapy, 46*, 314–322.

Rossetti, Y., Rode, G., Pisella, L., Farné, A., Li, L., Boisson, D., & Perenin, M. (1998). Prism adaptation to a rightward optical deviation rehabilitates left visuospatial neglect. *Nature, 395*, 166–169.

Rossi, P.W., Kheyfets, S. & Reding, M.J., (1990). Fresnel prisms improve visual perception in stroke patients with homonymous hemianopia or unilateral visual neglect. *Neurology, 40*, 1597–1599.

Rubens, A.B. (1985). Caloric stimulation and unilateral visual neglect. *Neurology, 35*, 1019–1024.

Sacks, O. (1983). *The man who mistook his wife for a hat*. Picador: Pan Books Ltd, UK.

Schenkenberg, T., Bradford, D.C., & Ajax, E.T. (1980). Line bisection and unilateral visual neglect patients with neurologic impairment. *Neurology, 30*, 509–517.

Serfaty, C., Soroker, N., Glicksohn, J., Sepkuti, J., & Myslobodsky, M.S. (1995). Does monocular viewing improve target detection in hemispatial neglect? *Restorative Neurology and Neuroscience, 9*, 77–83.

Seron, X., Deloche, G., & Coyette, F. (1989). A retrospective analysis of a single case neglect therapy: A point of theory. In X. Seron & G. Deloche (Eds.), *Cognitive approaches in neuropsychological rehabilitation*. Hillsdale, NJ: Lawrence Erlbaum Associates Inc.

Sheil, A. (1990). An investigation of the relationship between unilateral neglect and ADL dependencey. *Clinical Rehabilitation, 4*, 173–175.

Simms, B. (1985). Perception and driving: Theory and practice. *Occupational Therapy* (October), 363–366.

Sirigu, A; Grafman, J., Bressler, K., & Sunderland, T. (1991). Multiple representations contribute to body knowledge processing. *Brain, 114*, 629–642.

Sivak, M; Olsen, P.L., Kewman, D.G., Won, H., & Henson, D.L. (1981). Driving and perceptual/cognitive skills: Behavioural consequences of brain damage. *Archives of Physical Medicine and Rehabilitation, 62*, 476–483.

Söderback, I., Bengtsson, I., Ginsberg, E., & Ekholm, J. (1992). Video feedback in occupational therapy: Its effects in patients with neglect syndrome. *Archives of Physical Medicine and Rehabilitation, 73*, 1133–1139.

Sprague, J.M. (1996). Interaction of cortex and superior colliculus in mediation of visually guided behaviour in the cat. *Science, 153*, 1544–1547.

Starkstein, S.E., Fedoroff, J.P., Price, T.R., Leiguarda, R., & Robinson, R.G. (1993). Neuropsychological deficits in patients with anosognosia. *Neuropsychiatry, Neuropsychology and Behavioural Neurology, 6*, 43–48.

Sterzi, R., Bottini, G., Celani, M., Righetti, E., Lamassa, M., Ricci, M., & Vallar, G. (1993). Hemianopia, hemianaesthesia and hemiplegia after right and left hemisphere damage: A hemispheric difference. *Journal of Neurology, Neurosurgery and Psychiatry, 56*, 308–310.

Stone, S.P., Halligan, P.W., & Greenwood, R.J. (1993). The incidence of neglect phenomena and related disorders in patients with acute right or left hemisphere stroke. *Age and Aging, 23*, 46–52.

Stone, S.P., Halligan, P.W., Marshall, J.C., & Greenwood, R.J. (1998). Unilateral neglect: A common but heterogeneous syndrome. *Neurology, 50*, 1898–1901.

Stone, S.P., Halligan, P.W., Wilson, B., & Greenwood, R.J. (1991a). Performance of age matched controls on a battery of visuospatial neglect tests. *Journal of Neurology, Neurosurgery and Psychiatry, 55*, 341–344.

Stone, S.P., Patel, P., Greenwood, R.J., & Halligan, P.W. (1992). Measuring visual neglect in acute stroke and predicting its recovery: The visual neglect recovery index. *Journal of Neurology, Neurosurgery and Psychiatry, 55*, 431–436.

Stone, S.P., Wilson, B.A., Wroot, A., Halligan, P.W., Lange, L.S., Marshall, J.C. & Greenwood, R.J. (1991). The assessment of visuospatial neglect after acute stroke. *Journal of Neurology, Neurosurgery and Psychiatry, 54*, 345–350.

Taub, E., Miller, N.E., Novack, T.A., Cook, E.W., Fleming, W.C., Nepomuceno, C.S., Connell, J.S., & Crago, J.E. (1993). Technique to improve chronic motor deficit after stroke. *Archives of Physical Medicine and Rehabilitation, 74*, 347–354.

Tegnér, R., & Levander, M. (1991). Through the looking glass: A new technique to demonstrate dierctional hypokinesia in unilateral neglect. *Brain, 114*, 1943–1951.

Tham, K., & Tegnér, R. (1996). The baking task: A test of spatial neglect. *Neuropsychological Rehabilitation, 6*, 19–25.

Towle, D., & Lincoln, N.B. (1991a). Development of a questionnaire for detecting everyday problems in stroke patients with unilateral visual neglect. Clinical Rehabilitation, 5, 135–140.

Towle, D., & Lincoln, N.B. (1991b). Use of the Indented Paragraph test with right hemisphere-damaged stroke patients. *British Journal of Clinical Psychology, 30*, 37–45.

Trobe, J.D., Acosta, P.C., Krischer, J.P., & Trick, G.L. (1981). Confrontation visual field techniques in the detection of anterior visual pathway lesions. *Annals of Neurology, 10*, 28–34.

Turner, P. (1976). The place for CCTV in the rehabilitation of the low vision patient. *New Outlook Blind, 70*, 206–214.

Valenstein, E., & Heilman, K.M. (1981). Unilateral hypokinesia and motor extinction. *Neurology, 31*, 445–448.

Vallar, G., Antonucci, G., Guariglia, C., & Pizzamiglio, L. (1993). Deficits of position sense, unilateral neglect and optokinetic stimulation. *Neuropsychologia, 31*, 1191–1200.

Vallar, G., Bottini, G., Sterzi, R., Passerini, M.C., & Rusconi, M.L. (1991). Hemianesthesia, sensory neglect and defective access to conscious experience. *Neurology, 41*, 650–652.

Vallar, G., & Perani, D. (1986). The anatomy of unilateral neglect after right hemisphere stroke lesions: A clinical/CT-scan correlation study in man. *Neuropsychologia, 24*, 609–622.

Vallar, G., Rusconi, M.L., Barozzi, S., Bernardini, B., Ovadia, D., Papagno, C., & Cesarani, A. (1995). Improvement of left visuospatial hemineglect by left-sided transcutaneous electrical stimulation. *Neuropsychologia, 33*, 73–82.

Vallar, G., Rusconi, M.L., & Bernardini, B. (1996). Modulation of neglect hemianaesthesia by transcutaneous electrical stimulation. *Journal of the International Neuropsychological Society, 2*, 452–459.

Vallar, G., Sterzi, R., Bottini, G., Cappa, S., & Rusconi, M.L. (1990). Temporary remission of left hemianesthesia after vestibular stimulation: A sensory neglect phenomenon. *Cortex, 26*, 123–131.

Vuilleumier, P., Valenza, N., Mayer, E., Reverdin, A., & Landis, T. (1998). Near and far visual space in unilateral neglect. *Annals of Neurology, 43*, 406–410.

Wagenaar, R.C., Van Wieringen, P.C.W., Netelenbos, J.B., Meijer, O.G., & Kuik, D.J. (1992). The transfer of scanning training effects in visual attention after stroke: Five single case studies. *Disability and Rehabilitation, 14*, 51–60.

Walker, R., Findlay, J.M., Young, A.W., & Welch, J. (1991). Disentangling neglect and hemianopia. *Neuropsychologia, 29*, 1019–1027.

Walker, R., & Mattingley, J.B. (1997). Ghosts in the machine? Pathological visual completion phenomena in the damaged brain, *Neurocase, 3*, 313–336.

Walker, R., Young, A.W., & Lincoln, N. (1996). Eye patching and the rehabilitation of visual neglect. *Neuropsychological Rehabilitation, 6*, 219–231.

Webster, J., Jones, S., Blanton, P., Gross, R., Beissel, G., & Wofford, J. (1984). Visual scanning training with stroke patients. *Behaviour Therapy, 15*, 129–143.

Weinberg, J., Diller, L., Gordon, W., Gerstman, L., Lieberman, A., Lakin, P., Hodges, G., & Ezrachi, O. (1977). Visual scanning training effect on reading-related tasks in acquired right brain damage. *Archives of Physical Medicine and Rehabilitation, 58*, 479–486.

Weinstein, E.A. (1981). *Woodrow Wilson: A medical and psychological biography*. Princeton, NJ: Princeton University Press.

Weinstein, E.A., & Friedland, R. (Eds.) (1977a). Behavioural disorders associated with hemi-inattention. *Advances in neurology* (pp. 51–61). New York: Raven Press.

Weinstein, E., & Friedland, R. (1977b). *Hemi-inattention and hemispheric specialization*. New York: Raven Press.

Weintraub, S., & Mesulam, M. (1987). Right cerebral dominance in spatial attention: Further evidence based on ipsilateral neglect. *Archives of Neurology, 44*, 621–625.

Weintraub, S., & Mesulam, M. (1989). Neglect: Hemispheric specialisation, behavioural components and anatomical correlates. In F.J. Grafman (Eds.), *Handbook of neuropsychology* (pp. 357–374). Amsterdam: Elsevier Science Publishers.

Wertz, R.H., Goldberg, M.E., & Robinson, D.L. (1982). Brain mechanisms of visual attention. *Scientific American, 246*, 100–107.

Wiart, L., SaintCome, A.B., Debelleix, X., Petit, H., Joseph, P.A., & Mazaux, J.M. (1995). Unilateral neglect syndrome rehabilitation by trunk rotation and scanning training. *Archives of Physical Medicine and Rehabilitation, 78*, 424–429.

Wilson, B., Cockburn, J., & Halligan, P.W. (1987a). *The Behavioural Inattention Test*. Bury St. Edmunds, UK: Thames Valley Test Company.

Wilson, B., Cockburn, J., & Halligan, P.W. (1987b). Development of a behavioural test of visuospatial neglect. *Archives of Physical Medicine and Rehabilitation, 66*, 98–102.

Young, A.W., Hellawell, D., & Welch, J. (1992). Neglect and visual recognition. *Brain, 115*, 51–71.

Zarit, S., & Kahn, R. (1974). Impairment and adaption in chronic disabilities: Spatial inattention. *Journal of Nervous and Mental Diseases, 159*, 63–72.

Zoccolotti, P., & Judica, A. (1991). Functional evaluation of hemineglect by means of a semistructured scale: Personal extrapersonal differentiation. *Neuropsychological Rehabilitation, 1*, 33–44.

VIDEOS

Halligan, P.W., & Marshall, J.C. (1993). *Art and visuospatial perception: The effect of stroke on a graphic artist.* Hove, UK: Psychology Press (ISBN: 086377-3230).

Halligan, P.W. (1991). *Illustrations of visual neglect.* Hove, UK: Psychology Press (ISBN: 086377-3230).

Halligan, P.W. (1991). *The experience of visual neglect.* Hove, UK: Psychology Press (ISBN: 086377-3230).

Author Index

Acosta, P.C. 37
Ajax, E.T. 13
Albert, M. 79
Alexander, M. 60
André, J.-M. 86
Angelini, R. 68
Anton, H.A. 59, 86
Antonucci, G. 47, 64, 112, 139
Azouvi, P. 95

Babinski, J. 87
Barbut, D. 27
Barozzi, S. 136
Bartolomeo, P. 51
Battersby, W.S. 36
Beis, J.-M. 86–87
Beissel, G. 111
Bender, M.B. 36
Bengtsson, I. 132
Benowitz, L. 13
Bergego, C. 54, 95
Bernardini, B. 136
Berti, A. 13, 22, 60, 64
Beschin, N. 26, 68, 85, 96
Binder, J.R. 28

Bisiach, E. 13, 22, 26, 64, 68, 90, 106, 135
Blanton, P. 111
Blizzard, R.A. 98
Boisson, D. 141
Bottini, G. 35, 46–48, 136
Bowers, D. 22, 68
Bradford, D.C. 13
Bradshaw, J.A. 55
Bradshaw, J.L. 2, 55
Brechmann, M. 82
Bressler, K. 79
Brodie, E.E. 85
Brouchon, M. 28
Butter, C.M. 137–138

Calvanio, R. 13, 90, 108
Campbell, D.C. 55, 104
Caplan, B. 93–94
Caplan, L.R. 13, 35–36, 52, 64
Cappa, S. 46–47, 135
Cappa, S.F. 136
Carey, S.P. 53, 104
Cashman, E. 114
Celani, M. 35, 48
Cermak, S.A. 73

154

Cesarani, A. 136
Chamorro, A. 28
Chen Sea, M.J. 73
Cherington, M. 34
Christ, K. 136–137
Ciecierski, K. 28
Cocchini, G. 26, 68
Cockburn, J. 1, 11, 70, 79
Connell, J.S. 125
Cook, E.W. 125
Corwin, J.V. 139
Coslett, H.B. 22
Coughlan, T. 90
Coyette, F. 113
Crago, J.E. 125
Cubelli, R. 63
Cutting, J. 90–91

Daini, R. 96
Dana, DeWitt L. 52, 64
Debelleix, X. 128
Dehaut, F. 65
Della Sala, S. 26, 68
Deloche, G. 95, 113
Denes, G. 11, 13
Diller, L. 110, 113, 128
Donegan, C. 115–116
Doricchi, F. 28
Drasdo, N. 140
Driver, J. 33, 52
Drummond, A. 112, 127

Edgeworth, J. 68
Ekholm, J. 132
Ermino, F. 136
Ezrachi, O. 110

Fanthome, Y. 112, 127
Farné, A. 141
Fedoroff, J.P. 88, 90
Findlay, J.M. 42
Fischer, B. 128
Fitzpatrick, E. 22
Fleet, W.S. 52, 139
Fleming, W.C. 125
Ford, B. 3, 11–12
Fox, P.T. 130

Frackowiak, R.S.J. 136
Frasca, R. 52, 55, 105, 139
Friedland, R. 2, 58, 98
Friedman, P.J. 79
Friedrich, E.F. 137
Frith, C.D. 136
Fullerton, K.J. 13
Furukawa, T. 37, 43–44, 127

Gabellini, A.S. 63
Gainotti, G. 13, 51
Gallese, V. 26
Gardner, H. 17
Gassell, M.M. 48
Gauthier, L. 65
Gazzaniga, M. 27
Geggie, C. 123–124
Geminiani, G. 22, 90
Gerstman, L. 110
Gialanella, B. 13, 21, 131
Glicksohn, J. 137
Goldberg, M.E. 17
Goodale, M.A. 53, 55, 104–105
Goodman, J. 130
Gordon, W. 110
Grafman, J. 79
Greenwood, R.J. 13–14, 21, 34, 52, 81, 83, 90, 103
Gross, R. 111
Grossi, D. 68
Guariglia, C. 26, 28, 47, 64, 68, 112, 139

Haeske-Dewick, H. 96
Halligan, P.W. 1–2, 6, 11, 13–14, 17, 21–23, 26, 30–31, 33–34, 41, 44, 48–49, 51–52, 54, 60–64, 66–67, 70, 73, 79–83, 88, 90, 92, 95, 98, 103–105, 107, 115–119, 123
Harrer, M. 43
Hartje, W. 136–137
Hartman-Maeir, A. 77–78
Hashimoto, A. 139
Haws, B. 22
Heilman, K.M. 2, 14, 21–22, 24, 26, 39–41, 52, 65, 68, 139
Hellawell, D. 106

Subject Index